BROADVIEW PUBLIC LIBRARY DISTRICT
2226 SOUTH 16TH AVENUE
BROADVIEW, ILLINOIS 60153
(708) 345-1325

STATE REPORTS

The Great Plains

MONTANA ★ NEBRASKA ★ NORTH DAKOTA ★ SOUTH DAKOTA ★ WYOMING

By
John F. Grabowski
Patricia A. Grabowski

CHELSEA HOUSE PUBLISHERS
New York   Philadelphia

Produced by James Charlton Associates
New York, New York.

Copyright © 1992 by Chelsea House Publishers, a division of Main Line Book Co.
All rights reserved. Printed and bound in the United States of America.

First Printing

1   3   5   7   9   8   6   4   2

No part of this book may be reproduced or utilized in any form, or by any means, electronic or mechanical, including photocopying, recording, or by any information storage or retrieval system, without permission in writing from the publisher.

Library of Congress Cataloging-in-Publication Data

Grabowski, John F.
   The Great Plains : Montana, Nebraska, North Dakota, South Dakota, Wyoming / by John Grabowski, Patricia Grabowski.
   p. cm. — (State reports)
   Includes bibliographical references and index.
   Summary: Discusses the geographical, historical, and cultural aspects of Montana, Nebraska, North Dakota, South Dakota, and Wyoming.
   ISBN 0-7910-1052-X
        0-7910-1397-9 (pbk.)
   1. Great Plains—Juvenile literature. 2. West (U.S.)—Juvenile literature. [1. Great Plains. 2. Montana. 3. Nebraska. 4. North Dakota. 5. South Dakota. 6. Wyoming.] I. Grabowski, Patricia. II. Title. III. Series: Aylesworth, Thomas G. State reports.

F591.G67 1992   91-30784
917.8—dc20   CIP
                                     AC

Contents

Montana

State Seal, **5;** State Flag and Motto, **7;** State Capital, **9;** State Name and Nickname, **10;** State Flower, Tree, Bird, Animal, Fish, Gems, Grass, Slogan, and Songs, **10;** Population, **10;** Geography and Climate, **10;** Industries, **11;** Agriculture, **11;** Government, **11;** History, **11;** Sports, **12;** Major Cities, **13;** Places to Visit, **13;** Events, **13;** Famous People, **14;** Colleges and Universities, **14;** Where To Get More Information, **14.**

Nebraska

State Seal, **15;** State Flag and Motto, **17;** State Capital, **18;** State Name and Nicknames, **20;** State Flower, Tree, Bird, Day, Fossil, Insect, Gemstone, Grass, Mammal, Rock, Soil, Slogan, and Song, **20;** Population, **20;** Geography and Climate, **21;** Industries, **21;** Agriculture, **21;** Government, **21;** History, **21;** Sports, **23;** Major Cities, **23;** Places to Visit, **24;** Events, **24;** Famous People, **25;** Colleges and Universities, **26;** Where To Get More Information, **26.**

North Dakota

State Seal, **27;** State Flag and Motto, **29;** State Capital, **31;** State Name and Nicknames, **32;** State Flower, Tree, Bird, Art Gallery, Beverage, Fossil, Grass, March, and Song, **32;** Population, **32;** Geography and Climate, **33;** Industries, **33;** Agriculture, **33;** Government, **34;** History, **34;** Sports, **35;** Major Cities, **35;** Places to Visit, **36;** Events, **37;** Famous People, **38;** Colleges and Universities, **38;** Where To Get More Information, **38.**

South Dakota

State Seal, **39**; State Flag and Motto, **41**; State Capital, **43**; State Name and Nicknames, **44**; State Flower, Tree, Bird, Animal, Fish, Gem, Grass, Insect, Mineral, and Song, **44**; Population, **44**; Geography and Climate, **45**; Industries, **45**; Agriculture, **45**; Government, **45**; History, **46**; Sports, **47**; Major Cities, **48**; Places to Visit, **48**; Events, **49**; Famous People, **50**; Colleges and Universities, **50**; Where To Get More Information, **50**.

Wyoming

State Seal, **51**; State Flag and Motto, **53**; State Capital, **55**; State Name and Nicknames, **56**; State Flower, Tree, Bird, Gemstone, Mammal, and Song, **56**; Population, **56**; Geography and Climate, **56**; Industries, **57**; Agriculture, **57**; Government, **57**; History, **57**; Sports, **58**; Major Cities, **59**; Places to Visit, **59**; Events, **60**; Famous People, **61**; Colleges and Universities, **61**; Where To Get More Information, **61**.

Bibliography 62

Index 63

Montana

The state seal of Montana, adopted in 1893, depicts a landscape. A plow, pick, and shovel, symbolizing agriculture and mining, are in the foreground. Mountains, trees, and the Great Falls of the Missouri River in the background represent the state's natural beauty and resources. A ribbon with the state motto appears at the bottom. The border is inscribed "The Great Seal of the State of Montana."

State Flag
The state flag, adopted in 1905, consists of the design from the state seal centered on a bright blue field, with gold fringe borders in the upper and lower edges.

State Motto
Oro y Plata
The Spanish motto, which means "gold and silver," refers to the state's mineral resources.

Glacier National Park, created by Congress in 1910, lies in the Northern Rockies.

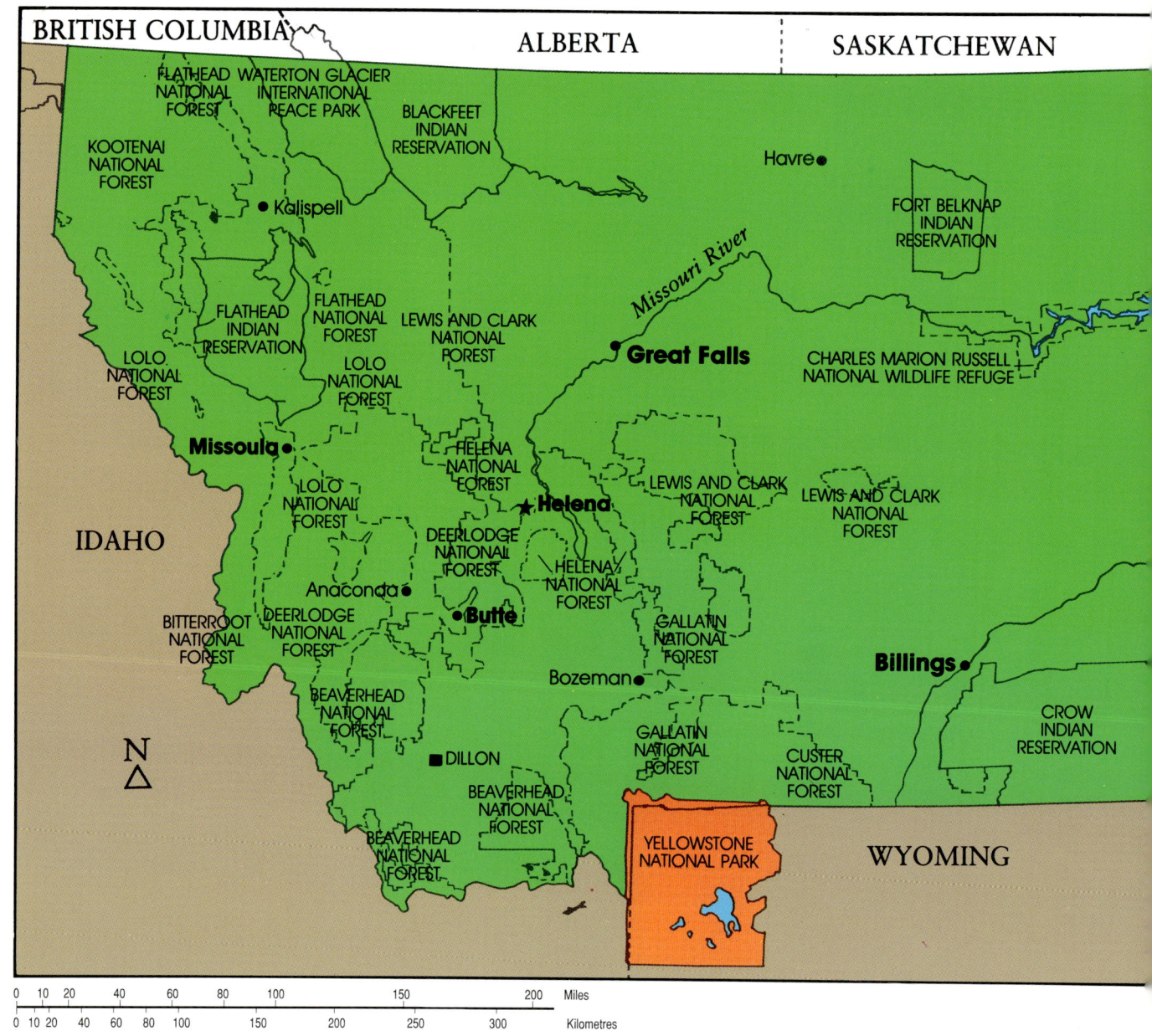

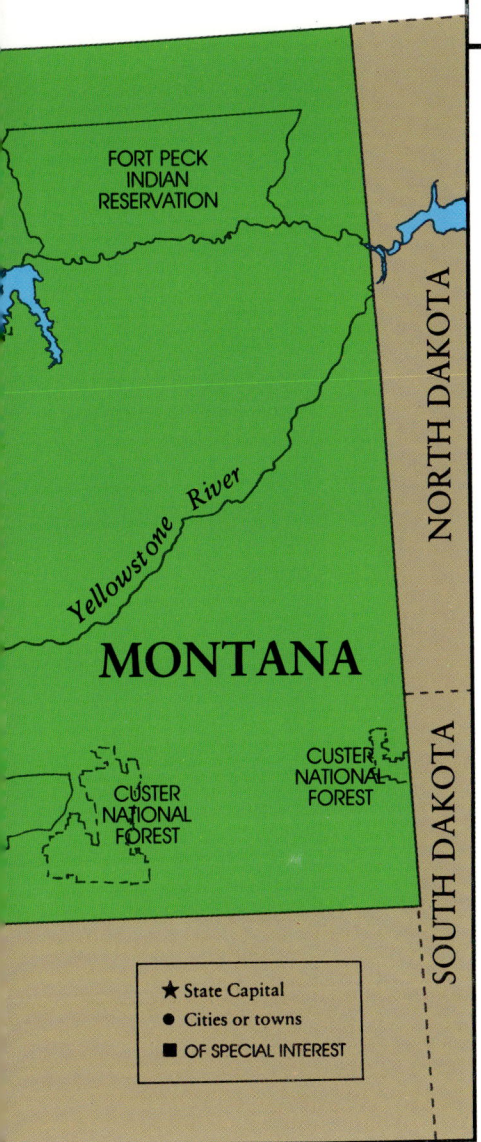

The state capitol in Helena holds paintings depicting Montana history.

State Capital

Helena has been the capital of Montana since 1875, fourteen years before statehood. The present capitol building, constructed of sandstone, was completed in 1902 at a cost of $485,000. The Greek neoclassical structure is crowned by a copper-clad dome. East and west wings were added between 1909 and 1912, and the building was altered somewhat during its reconstruction in 1963-65.

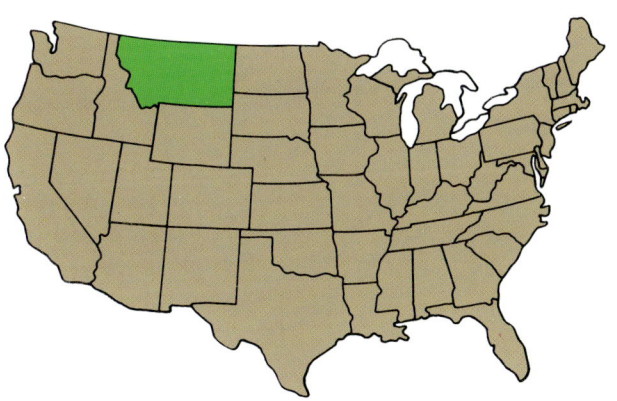

State Name and Nickname

The name Montana comes from the Spanish word *montaña*, meaning "mountain."

Montana is known as the *Big Sky Country* because of its large area of rugged mountains and valleys.

State Flower

Bitterroot, *Lewisia rediviva*, was named state flower in 1895, following a statewide vote conducted by the Montana Floral Emblem Association.

State Tree

In 1949, the ponderosa pine, *Pinus ponderosa*, was designated state tree.

State Bird

The western meadowlark, *Sturnella neglecta*, was adopted as state bird following a vote of schoolchildren.

State Animal

The grizzly bear, *Ursus arctos horribilis*, was chosen

The western meadowlark is the state bird.

state animal in 1983.

State Fish

In 1977, the blackspotted cutthroat trout, *Salmo clarki*, was selected state fish.

State Gems

The sapphire and Montana agate were named state gems in 1969.

State Grass

Bluebunch grass, *Agropyron spicatum*, was designated state grass in 1973.

State Slogan

The state slogan of Montana, "Naturally Inviting Montana," is used to promote tourism.

State Songs

"Montana," with words by Charles C. Cohen and music by Joseph E. Howard, was chosen state song in 1945. In the same year, "Montana Melody," written by Carleen and LeGrande Harvey, was named official state ballad.

Population

The population of Montana in 1990 was 803,655, making it the 44th most populous state. There are 5.5 people per square mile—52.9 percent of the population live in towns and cities.

Geography and Climate

Bounded on the north by the Canadian provinces of British Columbia, Alberta, and Saskatchewan; on the east by North and South Dakota; on the south by Wyoming and Idaho; and on the west by Idaho. Montana has an area of 147,046 square miles, making it the fourth

Montana

largest state. The state has a cold continental climate with low humidity. The Rocky Mountains cover the western third of the state, and the northern Great Plains makes up the eastern two-thirds. The highest point, at 12,799 feet, is Granite Peak in Park County, and the lowest point, at 1,800 feet, is along the Kootenai River in Lincoln County. The major waterways are the Bitterroot, Clark, Fork, Flathead, Kootenai, Marias, Milk, Missouri, Musselshell, Powder, Sun, and Yellowstone rivers. Flathead Lake is the largest natural lake in the state.

Industries

The principal industries of the state are agriculture, timber, mining, tourism, oil, and gas. The chief manufactured products are food products, wood and paper products, primary metals, printing and publishing, and petroleum and coal products.

Agriculture

The chief crops of the state are wheat, barley, sugar beets, hay, and oats. Montana is also a livestock state; there are estimated to be 2.35 million cattle, 245,000 hogs and pigs, 568,000 sheep, and 910,000 chickens and turkeys on its farms. Douglas fir, pines, and larch are harvested. Gold and copper are important mineral resources.

Government

The governor is elected to a four-year term, as are the lieutenant governor, attorney general, auditor, secretary of state, and superintendent of public instruction. The state legislature, which meets in odd-numbered years, consists of a 50-member senate and a 100-member house of representatives. Each of the 50 senatorial districts elects one senator to a four-year term, and each of the 100 representative districts elects one representative to a two-year term. The most recent state constitution was adopted in 1973. In addition to its two United States senators, Montana has one representative in the U.S. House of Representatives. The state has three votes in the electoral college.

History

Two groups of Indian tribes inhabited the Montana region before the arrival of the Europeans. The Arapaho, Assiniboin, Atsina, Blackfeet, Cheyenne, and Crow lived on the plains, while the Bannock, Kalispel, Kutenai, Salish, and Shoshone could be found in the mountains of the west. The Sioux, Mandan, and Nez Percé hunted throughout the region.

Fur trappers probably entered the Montana area in the 1740s. Following the Lewis and Clark expedition in 1805-06, fur trading expanded in the region. The first permanent settlement was built by the American Fur Company at Fort Benton in 1847. Most of eastern

Montana was acquired by the United States through the Louisiana Purchase in 1803, and the northwestern part was obtained through a treaty with Great Britain in 1846.

The discovery of gold on Grasshopper Creek in July 1862 spurred the growth of mining camps. These lawless towns prompted the formation of "vigilance committees," whose job it was to stop the thieving bands of outlaws. Congress created the Montana Territory in 1864, hoping that by strengthening local government the lawlessness would improve. During its territorial days, Montana was the site of "Custer's Last Stand." In this battle, which took place near the Little Bighorn River in 1876, the Sioux and Cheyenne Indians wiped out General George A. Custer and part of the 7th Cavalry.

Silver and copper mining began in the 1880s. Montana's population grew, railroads were built, and in 1889, Montana became the 41st state in the Union. During the early 1900s, dams built on the state's rivers provided electricity for new industries. Sugar refineries, flour mills, and meat-processing plants opened. In 1910, Congress established Glacier National Park, giving rise to the tourism industry.

Headstones mark the spots where George Custer and 210 of his men fell to the Sioux and Cheyenne on June 25, 1876.

The Great Depression of the 1930s hit Montana hard. The state's metals were no longer in demand, and a severe drought caused a drop in farm income. Federal and state projects provided jobs and much needed water for irrigation. During World War II, prosperity returned, with the state supplying copper and other metals to make war materials.

In the early 1950s, the oil industry expanded with the discovery of new oil fields in the Williston Basin. A $65-million aluminum plant began operating in 1955, providing an important new source of income.

Although agriculture remains essential to the state's economy, Montana is trying to encourage industrial growth, while striving to maintain its scenic beauty for the millions of tourists who visit each year.

Sports

Many sporting events on the collegiate and secondary

Montana

school levels are played throughout the state. Montana offers vast opportunities for almost every kind of outdoor sport. Summer recreational activities include boating, water skiing, biking, horseback riding, mountain climbing, and pack trips into wilderness areas. Montana's most popular winter sport in skiing.

Major Cities

Billings (population 66,798). Founded in 1882 by the Northern Pacific Railway, Montana's largest city lies on the west bank of the Yellowstone River. Today, it is a major trade center for the region. Agriculture, tourism, and oil are the city's main industries.

Things to see in Billings:
Chief Black Otter Trail, Range Rider of the Yellowstone, Boothill Cemetery, Yellowstone Art Center, Peter Yegen Jr. Museum, Western Heritage Center, Indian Caves.

Helena (population 23,938). Settled in 1864, the town was originally called Last Chance Gulch after four discouraged prospectors explored the area as their "last chance" to find gold. Eventually the gulch and the area around it produced $20 million in gold. Renamed Helena, it was designated state capital in 1894. Agriculture, smelting, and ore refining are important to the city's economy.

Things to see in Helena:
State Capitol, Montana Historical Society Museum, Original Governor's Mansion, Holter Museum of Art, Pioneer Cabin (1864), Gates of the Mountains, and Frontier Town.

Places to Visit

The National Park Service maintains seven areas in the state of Montana: Big Hole National Battlefield, Custer Battlefield National Monument, Glacier National Park, Fort Union Trading Post National Historic Site, Grant-Kohrs Ranch National Historic Site, three of the five entrances to Yellowstone National Park, and part of the Bighorn Canyon National Recreation Area. There are also 26 state recreation areas.

Chinook: Chief Joseph Battleground State Monument. This is the site of the last battle between the U.S. Army and the Nez Percé Indians.

Drummond: Bearmouth Ghost Town. Visitors are invited to search for a baking powder can containing a fortune, which is supposedly buried here.

Great Falls: Charles M. Russell Museum Complex and Original Studio. The museum features the work of cowboy artist Charles M. Russell.

Whitehall: Lewis and Clark Caverns State Park. The limestone cavern located in this 2,735-acre park contains intricate passageways and multicolored formations.

Events

There are many events and organizations that schedule activities of various kinds in the state of Montana. Here are some of them.

Sports: NRA/MRA Rodeo (Big Timber), College National Finals Rodeo (Bozeman), Montana Pro Rodeo Circuit Finals (Great Falls), Governor's Cup Sled Dog Races (Helena), Copper Cup Regatta (Polson), Great American Ski Chase (West

Yellowstone), Wild Horse Stampede (Wolf Point).

Arts and Crafts: Festival of the Arts (Big Fork), Threshing Bee and Antique Show (Culbertson).

Music: Traditional Jazz Festival (Helena), Montana State Fiddlers' Contest (Polson), Music Festival (Red Lodge).

Entertainment: Montana Fair (Billings), Northern International Livestock Exposition Spring Show (Billings), Midland Empire Horse Show (Billings), Montana Winter Fair (Bozeman), Festival of Nations (Butte), Harvest Festival (Glasgow), Northeast Montana Fair and Rodeo (Glasgow), State Fair (Great Falls), Little Big Horn Days (Hardin), Crow Fair (Hardin), Havre Festival Days (Havre), Vigilante Parade (Helena), Governor's Cup All-Breeds Horse Show (Helena), Agriculture-Farm Show (Kalispell), Glacier International Horse Show (Kalispell), Libby Logger Days and River Races (Libby), Nordicfest (Libby), Park County Fair and O'Mok-See (Livingston), Milk River Wagon Train (Malta), Western Montana Quarter Horse Show (Missoula), Festival of Nations (Red Lodge), Opeta-Ye-Teca Indian Celebration (Wolf Point).

Tours: Yellowstone River Float Trip (Billings), Old No. 1 (Butte), Last Chancer Tour Train (Helena).

Theater: Bigfork Summer Playhouse (Bigfork), Montana Cowboy Poetry Gathering (Big Timber), Fort Peck Summer Theater (Glasgow), Old Opera House (Virginia City), Playmill Theater (West Yellowstone).

Famous People

Many famous people were born in the state of Montana. Here are a few:

Dirk Benedict b. 1945, Helena. Television actor: *Battlestar Galactica, The A-Team*

Gary Cooper 1901-61, Helena. Two-time Academy Award-winning film actor: *Sergeant York, High Noon*

Patrick Duffy b. 1949, Townsend. Television actor: *Dallas*

Chet Huntley 1911-74, Cardwell. Radio and television journalist

Phil Jackson b. 1945, Deer Lodge. Basketball player and coach

Myrna Loy b. 1905, Helena. Film actress: *The Thin Man, The Best Years of Our Lives*

David Lynch b. 1946, Missoula. Television and film director: *Twin Peaks, The Elephant Man*

Jeannette Rankin 1880-1973, near Missoula. Suffragist and first woman member of Congress

Colleges and Universities

There are many colleges and universities in Montana. Here are the more prominent, with their locations, dates of founding, and enrollments.

Eastern Montana College, Billings, 1927, 4,055

Montana College of Mineral Science and Technology, Butte, 1893, 1,771

Montana State University, Bozeman, 1893, 10,251

University of Montana, Missoula, 1893, 9,679

Where To Get More Information

Montana Travel Promotion Division
Department of Commerce
1424 9th Avenue
Helena, MT 59620
1-800-548-3390

Nebraska

Pictured in the center of the state seal is a blacksmith at work, representing the mechanical arts; a settlers' cabin, stacks of corn, and sheaves of wheat, symbolizing agriculture; and a steamboat and train, representing transportation. The Rocky Mountains can be seen in the distance, and a ribbon containing the state motto floats above them. The border around the seal reads "Great Seal of the State of Nebraska" and "March 1st, 1867"—the date of the state's admission to the Union.

State Flag

The state flag, which was adopted in 1963, consists of the state seal printed in gold and silver on a dark blue field.

State Motto

Equality Before the Law

This motto, adopted in 1867, refers to one of the basic principles of the American system of justice.

A hay field stretches under the blue Nebraska sky.

Nebraska

The state capitol in Lincoln is known as the Tower of the Plains.

State Capital

Lincoln has been the capital since 1867, the year Nebraska became a state. The modern, two-story capitol building was built of Indiana limestone and completed in 1932 at a cost of more than $10 million. Its central tower, which reaches a height of 400 feet, is crowned by a bronze statue entitled "The Sower."

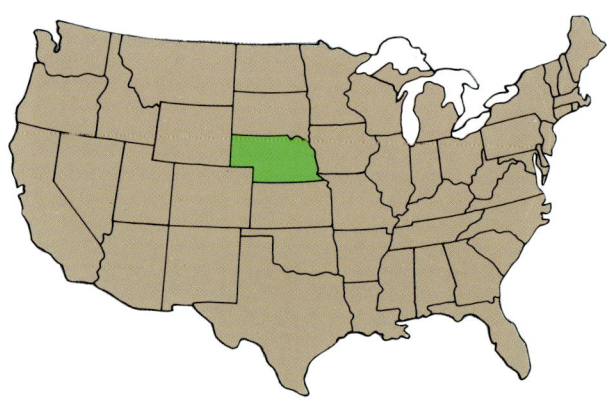

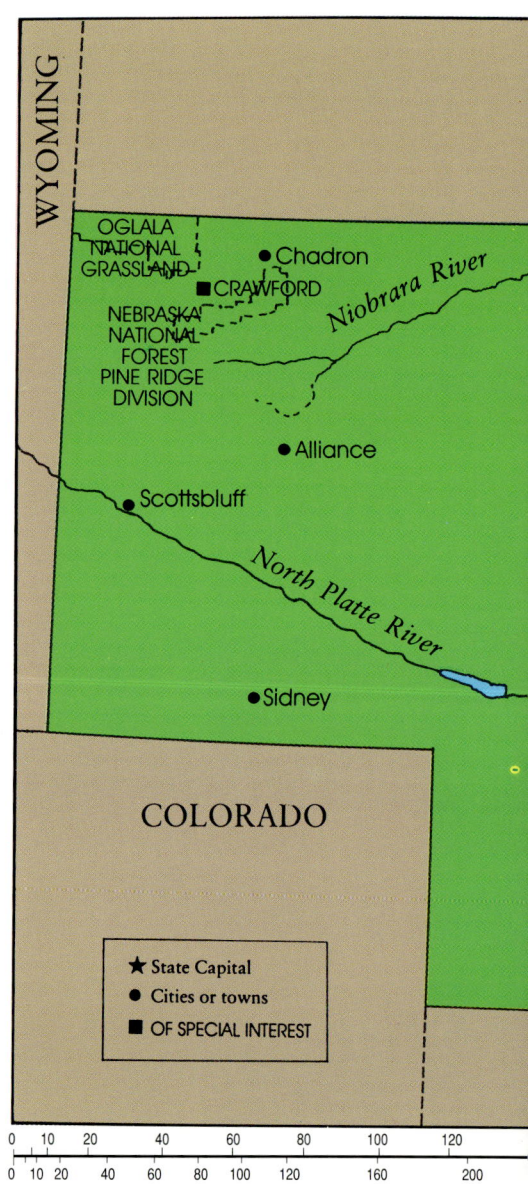

Nebraska

State Name and Nicknames

The name Nebraska comes from the Omaha Indian word *Nebrathka*, meaning "flat water." It referred to the Platte River.

The *Cornhusker State*, Nebraska's official nickname since 1945, refers to the method of harvesting, or "husking," corn. It was changed from the *Tree Planters' State,* which had been adopted in 1895. Unofficial nicknames include the *Antelope State* for its many herds of antelope, and the *Bug-Eating State* for its many bug-eating bull bats.

State Flower

Goldenrod, *Solidago serotina*, was selected as state flower in 1895.

State Tree

In 1972, the cottonwood, *Populus deltoides*, was adopted as state tree.

State Bird

The western meadowlark, *Sturnella neglecta*, was named state bird in 1929.

State Day

March 1 was designated state day in 1931.

State Fossil

The mammoth was selected state fossil in 1967.

State Insect

The honeybee, *apis mellifera*, was chosen state insect in 1975.

State Gemstone

Blue agate was designated state gemstone in 1967.

Goldenrod is the state flower.

State Grass

Little bluestem was named official state grass in 1969.

State Mammal

In 1981, the white-tailed deer, *Cariacus virginianus*, was selected state mammal.

State Rock

Prairie agate was named state rock in 1967.

State Soil

The state soil of Nebraska is typic arguistolls.

State Slogan

"Welcome to Nebraskaland, where the West begins," was designated state slogan in 1963.

State Song

"Beautiful Nebraska," with music by Jim Fras and words by Jim Fras and Guy G. Miller, was adopted as state song in 1967.

Population

The population of Nebraska in 1990 was 1,584,617, making

Nebraska

it the 36th most populous state. There are 20.5 people per square mile—62.9 percent of the population live in towns and cities.

Geography and Climate

Bounded on the north by South Dakota, on the east by Iowa and Missouri, on the south by Kansas and Colorado, and on the west by Colorado and Wyoming, Nebraska has an area of 77,355 square miles, making it the 15th largest state. The climate is continental semi-arid. The plains of the central lowland cover the eastern one-third of the state, while the Great Plains and hill country comprise the remainder. The highest point, at 5,426 feet, is in Johnson Township in Kimball County, and the lowest point, at 840 feet, is along the Missouri River in Richardson County. The major waterways are the Missouri, Platte, North Platte, South Platte, Loup, Elkhorn, Republican, Big Blue, Little Blue, and Niobrara rivers. Lake McConaughy, the state's largest lake, is man-made.

Industries

The principal industries of the state are agriculture and food processing. The chief manufactured products are foods, machinery, electric and electronic equipment, primary and fabricated metal products, and transportation equipment.

Agriculture

The chief crops of the state are corn, sorghum, soybeans, hay, wheat, beans, oats, potatoes, and sugar beets. Nebraska is also a livestock state; there are estimated to be 5.5 million cattle, 4 million hogs and pigs, 180,000 sheep, and 4.5 million chickens and turkeys on its farms. Portland cement, crushed stone, and construction sand and gravel are important mineral resources.

Government

The governor is elected to a four-year term, as are the secretary of state, attorney general, treasurer, and auditor. Nebraska is the only state whose legislature consists of one house. Its 49 members, called senators, are elected from 49 legislative districts and serve four-year terms. This unicameral legislature meets annually. The most recent state constitution was adopted in 1875. In addition to its two United States senators, Nebraska has three representatives in the U. S. House of Representatives. The state has five votes in the electoral college.

History

Several Indian tribes inhabited the Nebraska area when the Europeans arrived. The Missouri, Omaha, Oto, and Ponca Indians farmed and hunted along the rivers; the Pawnee, on the plains. The Arapaho, Cheyenne, Comanche, and Sioux were wandering tribes who hunted in western Nebraska. Other tribes, driven from their lands

The Oregon Trail, which carried thousands of travelers through Nebraska, was one of the most famous wagon trails in the history of the West.

by white settlers, moved into the area. The Fox, Iowa, and Sauk arrived in the 1830s, the Santee Sioux in 1863, and the Winnebago in 1863-64.

Both Spain and France claimed present-day Nebraska at various times. The Spanish claim was based on the explorations of Francisco Vásquez de Coronado in 1541.

Nebraska was also part of the Louisiana Territory claimed by Robert Cavelier, Sieur de la Salle, for France in 1682. France sold the land to the United States as part of the Louisiana Purchase in 1803. The following year, Meriwether Lewis and William Clark explored eastern Nebraska. Zebulon M. Pike, another American explorer, entered the area in 1806. Traveling eastward from Oregon in 1812, fur agent Robert Stuart followed a route along the Platte River that would later become known as the Oregon Trail. In 1819, the U. S. Army established Fort Atkinson near present-day Omaha. Although it was abandoned in 1827, it was the site of Nebraska's first school, library, sawmill, grist mill, and brickyard.

The year 1843 marked the beginning of the "Great Migration," which brought thousands of pioneers along the Oregon Trail through Nebraska to Washington and Oregon. Until 1854, when Congress created the Nebraska Territory, the area had been maintained as Indian country. In 1862, the first Homestead Act, granting free land to settlers, brought thousands of people to Nebraska. By 1870, the population numbered 122,993. Nebraska was admitted to the Union as the 37th state in 1867.

The state's growth was slowed between 1874 and 1877 because of huge swarms of grasshoppers that severely damaged farmers' crops. Many people abandoned their farms and returned East. In 1890, the state was hit by drought, and again many farmers lost their land. During the early 1900s, the federal government funded the North Platte Project to provide water for irrigation.

Nebraska suffered greatly during the Great Depression of the 1930s. A severe drought hit, and prices for farm products fell. In 1934, voters approved a change to a unicameral, or one-house, legislature.

Nebraska

Oil was discovered in southeastern Nebraska in 1939. It quickly became the state's most important mineral. World War II brought prosperity to Nebraska's farmers, who provided corn, oats, potatoes, and wheat to meet the wartime food shortages.

Today, despite the growth of manufacturing, agriculture remains important to the state's economy.

Sports

Many sporting events on the collegiate and secondary school levels are played throughout the state. In football, the University of Nebraska is a perennial power, having won the Orange Bowl in 1964, 1971, 1972, 1973, and 1983; the Sugar Bowl in 1974, 1985, and 1987; and the Cotton Bowl in 1974.

Although the state does not have any professional teams in the major sports leagues, the Omaha Racers are members of the Continental Basketball Association, which is the official developmental league of the National Basketball Association.

Major Cities

Lincoln (population 171,932). When Lincoln was named state capital in 1867, only thirty people lived in the town. By the mid-1870s, the population had grown to 2,500, and public utilities, a capitol building, a railroad line, and a university had been built. Today, Lincoln is the state's second largest city, as well as a major grain market and center for manufacturing, finance, and trade.

Things to see in Lincoln: State Capitol, Lincoln Monument, Executive Mansion, University of Nebraska State Museum, Encounter Center, Lentz Center for Asian Culture, Ralph Mueller Planetarium, Sheldon Memorial Art Gallery and Sculpture Garden, Christlieb Collection of Western Art, Elder Art Gallery, Museum of Nebraska History, William Jennings Bryan Home (1902), Statehood Memorial—Thomas P. Kennard House (1869), Ferguson Mansion (1910), National Museum of Roller Skating, Folsom Children's Zoo, and Robber's Cave.

The city of Lincoln sits in a basin fifty miles south of the Platte River. The first railroad arrived in the state capital in 1870.

Omaha (population 313,911). Nebraska's largest city was founded in 1854, after the Omaha Indians signed a treaty with the federal government and left the area. The city soon became a supply center for wagon trains and prospectors headed west. Today, in addition to being home to the headquarters of the Strategic Air Command, Omaha is one of the largest livestock markets and meat-packing centers of the world.

Things to see in Omaha: Joslyn Art Museum, Great Plains Black Museum, Omaha Children's Museum, Union Pacific Historical Museum, Old Market, Mutual of Omaha Dome, Henry Doorly Zoo, Western Heritage Museum/Omaha History Museum, Gerald Ford Birth Site, Mormon Pioneer Cemetery, Ak-Sar-Ben Field and Coliseum, Boys Town, Historic Bellevue, Strategic Air Command Museum, Fontenelle Forest, USS *Hazard*, USS *Marlin*, and St. Cecilia's Cathedral.

Places to Visit

The National Park Service maintains four areas in the state of Nebraska: Scotts Bluff National Monument, Homestead National Monument of America, Agate Fossil Beds National Monument, and Chimney Rock National Historic Site. In addition, there are 57 state recreation areas.

Auburn: Brownville. Visitors may tour restored buildings, including Dr. Spurgin's Dental Office and the Brownville Depot, in this riverboat town of the 1800s.

Chadron: Museum of the Fur Trade. Displays featuring frontier weapons, tanning equipment, and furs, trace the history of the nineteenth-century fur trade on the Missouri River.

Gothenburg: Pony Express Station. Originally located on the Oregon Trail, this building was used by the Pony Express from 1860 to 1861.

Hastings: Hastings Museum. Exhibits in this museum include mineral displays, Indian items, and pioneer artifacts.

Minden: Harold Warp Pioneer Village. This 26-building complex features an 1869 Indian fort, a pony express station, a general store, and a sod house.

Nebraska City: John Brown's Cave. This major stop of the Underground Railway was run by the great abolitionist.

North Platte: Buffalo Bill Ranch State Historical Park. This ranch, which includes an 18-room house and a barn, was the home of William F. Cody.

Red Cloud: Willa Cather Historical Center. Visitors may tour the childhood home of the author, and view exhibits on her life.

Events

There are many events and organizations that schedule activities of various kinds in the state of Nebraska. Here are some of them.

Sports: Little Britches State Rodeo (Chadron), horse racing at Agricultural Park (Columbus), Johnson Lake Yacht Club Annual Regatta (Lexington), Sailing Regatta (McCook), Buffalo Bill Rodeo (North Platte), Ogallala Round-up Rodeo (Ogallala), Governor's Cup Sailing Regatta (Ogallala), NCAA College Baseball World Series (Omaha), World's Championship Rodeo (Omaha), Old West Balloon Rally (Scottsbluff), Missouri River Raft

Nebraska

Regatta (South Sioux City), horse racing at Atokad Park (South Sioux City).

Arts and Crafts: Art in the Park Arts Festival (Kearney), Antique and Crafts Extravaganza (Lexington), Lincoln Gem and Mineral Club Show (Lincoln), Arbor Day Arts Festival (Nebraska City), Spring Festival of Crafts (Norfolk), Omaha Summer Arts Festival (Omaha), Orchid Show and Sale (Omaha).

Music: Flatwater Festival (Lincoln), Lincoln Symphony Orchestra (Lincoln), Nebraska Chamber Orchestra (Lincoln), Omaha Ballet (Omaha), Omaha Symphony (Omaha), Nebraska Choral Arts Society (Omaha), Nebraska State Country Music Championship (Springfield).

Entertainment: Homestead Days (Beatrice), "Gateway to the West" Days (Blair), Fur Trade Days (Chadron), Buckskin Rendezvous (Chadron), Lewis and Clark Tri-State Dairy Expo (Crofton), Northeast Nebraska Cow Chip Flip (Crofton), Crystal Springs Camp-in (Fairbury), Old Settlers Celebration and Parade (Fremont), John C. Frémont Days (Fremont), Oregon Trail Days (Gering), Pony Express Harvest Festival (Gothenburg), Nebraska Antique Airplane Association Fly-in (Gothenburg), Husker Harvest Days (Grand Island), Harvest of Harmony Festival and Parade (Grand Island), Swedish Days (Holdredge), Old Fashioned Fourth of July (Lexington), Camp Creek Antique Machinery and Threshing Association Festival (Lincoln), National Czech Festival (Lincoln), Nebraska State Fair (Lincoln), LaVitsef Celebration (Norfolk), Nebraskaland Days Celebration (North Platte), Indian Summer Rendezvous (Ogallala), River City Round-up (Omaha), Christmas at Union Station (Omaha), Fort Sidney Days and Rod 'n Roll (Sidney), Chicken Show (Wayne).

Tours: Oregon Trail Wagon Train (Bayard), *The Spirit of Brownville* cruises (Brownville), Tour of the Frank House (Kearney).

Theaters: Village Theater (Auburn), Post Playhouse (Crawford), Lincoln Community Playhouse (Lincoln), Christmas Pageant and Lights (Minden), Omaha Community Playhouse (Omaha), Orpheum Theater (Omaha), Emmy Gifford Children's Theater (Omaha).

Famous People

Many famous people were born in the state of Nebraska. Here are a few:

Grover Cleveland Alexander 1887-1950, Elba. Hall of Fame baseball pitcher

Fred Astaire 1899-1987, Omaha. Dancer and film actor: *The Gay Divorcée, Silk Stockings*

Nebraska celebrates part of its immigrant history every year at the National Czech Festival in Lincoln.

Max Baer 1909-59, Omaha. Heavyweight boxing champion

Wade Boggs b. 1958, Omaha. Baseball player

Marlon Brando b. 1924, Omaha. Two-time Academy Award-winning actor: *On the Waterfront, The Godfather*

Richard B. Cheney b. 1941, Lincoln. Secretary of Defense

Montgomery Clift 1920-66, Omaha. Film actor: *Red River, From Here to Eternity*

Sam Crawford 1880-1968, Wahoo. Hall of Fame baseball player

Sandy Dennis b. 1937, Hastings. Academy Award-winning film actress: *Who's Afraid of Virginia Woolf?*

Loren Eiseley 1907-77, Lincoln. Anthropologist

Henry Fonda 1905-82, Grand Island. Academy Award-winning film actor: *On Golden Pond, The Grapes of Wrath*

Gerald Ford b. 1913, Omaha. Thirty-eighth President of the United States

Bob Gibson b. 1935, Omaha. Hall of Fame baseball pitcher

Swoosie Kurtz b. 1944, Omaha. Tony Award-winning stage and television actress: *Fifth of July; Love, Sydney*

Harold Lloyd 1893-1971, Burchard. Actor and film producer

Malcolm X 1925-65, Omaha. Religious leader

Nick Nolte b. 1940, Omaha. Film actor: *48 HRS, The Deep*

Red Cloud 1822-1909, north-central Nebraska. Indian leader

Robert Taylor 1911-69, Filley. Film actor: *Magnificent Obsession, Johnny Eager*

Darryl Zanuck 1902-79, Wahoo. Motion picture producer

Colleges and Universities

There are many colleges and universities in Nebraska. Here are the more prominent, with their locations, dates of founding, and enrollments.

Bellevue College, Bellevue, 1965, 1,956

Chadron State College, Chadron, 1911, 2,850

College of Saint Mary, Omaha, 1923, 1,127

Creighton University, Omaha, 1878, 6,068

Nebraska Wesleyan University, Lincoln, 1887, 1,607

Peru State College, Peru, 1867, 1,835

University of Nebraska at Kearney, Kearney, 1903, 9,745; *at Omaha,* Omaha, 1908, 15,305; *at Lincoln,* Lincoln, 1869, 23,926; *Medical Center,* Omaha, 1869, 2,405

Wayne State College, Wayne, 1891, 3,324

Where To Get More Information

Nebraska Travel and Tourism Division
P.O. Box 94666
Lincoln, NE 68509
1-800-228-4307

North Dakota

The state seal of North Dakota, adopted in 1889, shows an elm tree surrounded by three sheaves of wheat, a plow, an anvil, and a sledge, representing agriculture. A bow, three arrows, and an Indian on horseback chasing a buffalo symbolize the tribes that lived in the region. The state motto and 42 stars appear in a semicircle around the top. In the border surrounding the seal is printed "Great Seal, State of North Dakota" and "October 1st, 1889."

State Flag

The state flag of North Dakota, adopted in 1911, contains a bald eagle with spread wings carrying an olive branch and arrows in its talons. In its beak is a scroll that reads *E Pluribus Unum* (one out of many). The design, centered on a blue background, resembles the coat of arms of the United States. A scroll with the state name appears at the bottom of the flag. Above the eagle is a double semicircle of stars representing the original 13 states.

State Motto

Liberty and Union, Now and Forever, One and Inseparable

This quotation from Daniel Webster's "Reply to Hayne" was adopted as state motto in 1889.

Lake Sakakawea is one of many that dot the North Dakota landscape.

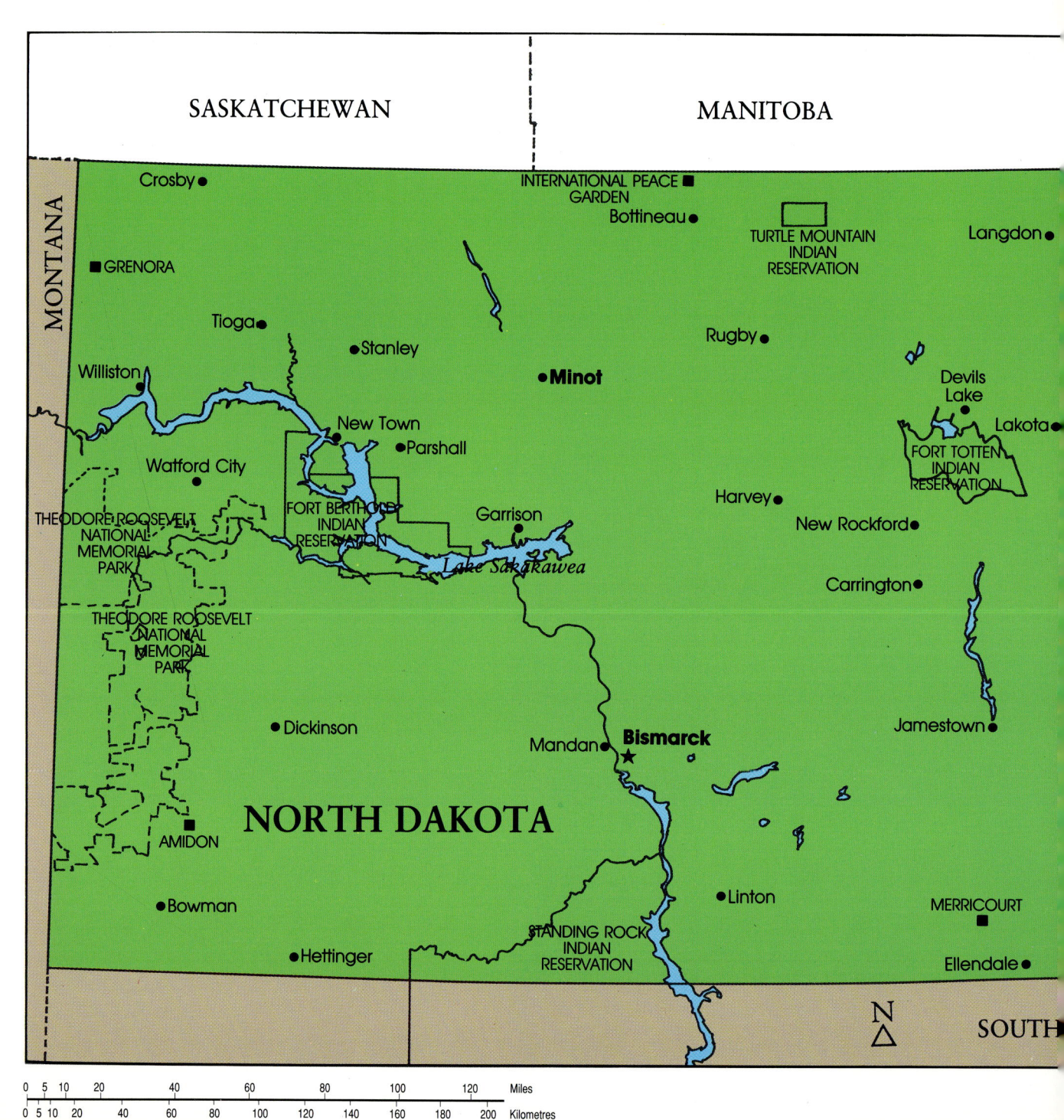

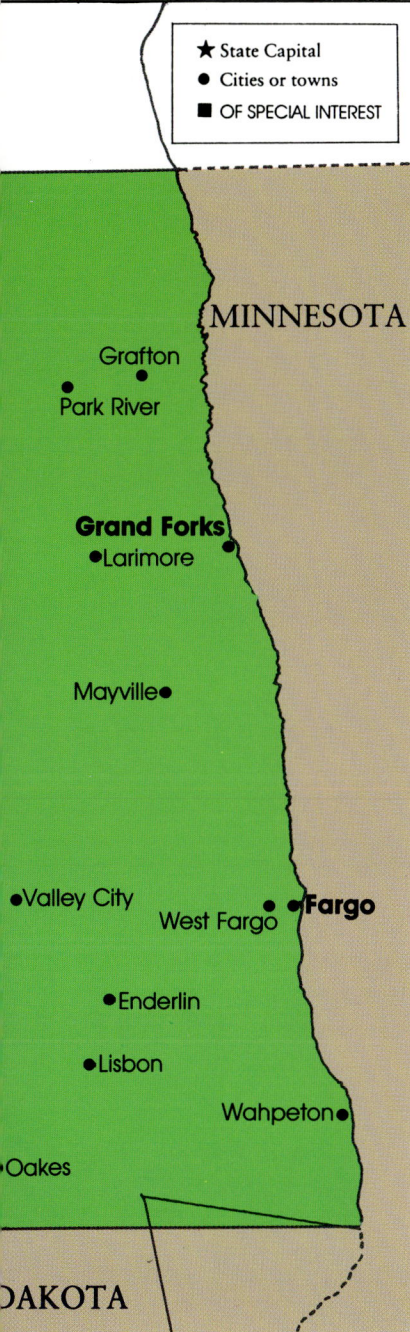

State Capital

Bismarck became the territorial capital in 1883 and the state capital in 1889, when North Dakota entered the Union. The present capitol building was completed in 1934 at a cost of $2 million. The 19-story, modern structure, built of Indiana limestone, was renovated between 1971 and 1981 at a cost of more than $10 million. A four-story judicial wing and state office building were added in the 1970s.

The capitol in Bismarck was constructed for a mere $2 million after the first capitol building burned down in 1930.

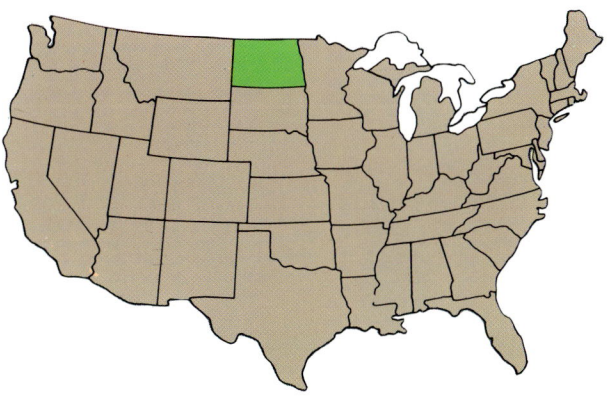

State Name and Nicknames

North Dakota was named for the Sioux Indians, who called themselves *Dakota* or *Lakota*, which meant "allies" or "friends."

North Dakota's two official nicknames are the *Sioux State* and the *Flickertail State*. They refer to the Sioux Indians that inhabited the area and to the state's large population of flickertail ground squirrels. North Dakota is also known as the *Peace Garden State* for the International Peace Garden, which lies on its border with Manitoba.

State Flower

In 1907, the state legislature selected the wild prairie rose, *Rosa blanda* or *Rosa arkansana*, as state flower.

The state flower is the wild prairie rose.

State Tree

The American elm, *Ulmus americana*, was chosen state tree in 1947.

State Bird

The western meadowlark, *Sturnella neglecta*, was designated state bird in 1947.

State Art Gallery

In 1981, the University of North Dakota Art Gallery, on the Grand Forks campus, was selected state art gallery.

State Beverage

Milk was named state beverage in 1983.

State Fossil

Teredo petrified wood was chosen state fossil in 1967.

State Grass

In 1977, western wheat grass, *Agropyron smithii*, was designated state grass.

State March

In 1975, "Spirit of the Land,"

The western meadowlark is the state bird.

written by James D. Ployhar, was adopted as state march.

State Song

"North Dakota Hymn," with words by James W. Foley and music by C. S. Putnam, was named state song in 1947.

Population

The population of North Dakota in 1990 was 641,364, making it the 47th most populous state. There are 9.1 people per square mile—48.8 percent of the population live in towns and cities.

North Dakota

Geography and Climate

Bounded on the north by the Canadian provinces of Saskatchewan and Manitoba, on the east by Minnesota, on the south by South Dakota, and on the west by Montana, North Dakota has an area of 70,702 square miles, making it the 17th largest state. The climate is continental, with wide-ranging temperatures and moderate rainfall. The three main land regions include the Red River Valley in the east, the Drift Prairie in the central portion of the state, and the Great Plains in the southwest. The highest point, at 3,506 feet, is White Butte in Slope County, and the lowest point, at 750 feet, is along the Red River in Pembina County. The major waterways are the Missouri, Red, Cannonball, Heart, Knife, Little Missouri, James, Goose, Park, Pembina, Sheyenne, and Souris rivers. Devils Lake is the state's largest natural lake.

The Badlands were created over three million years by water flooding soft sediments and volcanic ash.

Industries

The principal industries of the state are agriculture, mining, manufacturing, and tourism. The chief manufactured products are farm equipment, and processed foods.

Agriculture

The chief crops of the state are spring wheat, durum,

barley, rye, flaxseed, oats, potatoes, dried edible beans, honey, soybeans, sugar beets, sunflowers, and hay. North Dakota is also a livestock state; there are estimated to be 2 million cattle, 285,000 hogs and pigs, 180,000 sheep, and 1.4 million chickens and turkeys on its farms. Lime, construction sand and gravel, and crushed stone are important mineral resources.

Government

The governor is elected to a four-year term, as are the lieutenant governor, attorney general, secretary of state, treasurer, auditor, and superintendent of public instruction. The state legislature, which meets in odd-numbered years, consists of a 53-member senate and a 106-member house of representatives. Forty-nine of the 53 legislative districts elect one senator and two representatives. For voting purposes, the remaining four are grouped into two districts, each of which elects two senators and four representatives. Senators serve four-year terms, and representatives serve two-year terms. In addition to its two United States senators, North Dakota has one representative in the U. S. House of Representatives. The state has three votes in the electoral college.

History

Before the Europeans arrived in present-day North Dakota, the Arikara, Cheyenne, Hidatsa, and Mandan tribes farmed the land in the Missouri Valley. The Assiniboin, Chippewa, and Sioux were hunters and warriors who lived in the northeastern part of the region.

Robert Cavelier, Sieur de la Salle, claimed the southwestern half of the area for France in 1682. France

Fort Totten is a well-preserved frontier military outpost that was established on the shore of Devils Lake in July 1867.

North Dakota

also claimed the northeastern part, but gave it to Great Britain in 1713. In 1738, Pierre Gaultier de Varennes, Sieur de la Vérendrye, made the first explorations of the region as he traveled from Canada to the Mandan Indian villages in south-central North Dakota.

In 1803, France sold the land west of the Mississippi to the United States. The next year, Meriwether Lewis and William Clark explored the Louisiana Territory, as this area was named, on their way to the Pacific Ocean. The first permanent settlement was established at Pembina in 1812 by Scottish and Irish families from Canada. The United States acquired northeastern North Dakota by an 1818 treaty with Great Britain.

In 1861, Congress established the Dakota Territory, which included the present states of North and South Dakota and a large part of Montana and Wyoming. Although the territory was opened for homesteading in 1863, large numbers of settlers did not arrive until the 1870s and 1880s, after the fear of Indian attacks had lessened. Around 1875, "bonanza" farming developed. These large, profitable farms employed machinery and orderly methods of planting, harvesting, and marketing. Cattle raising also became an important industry at this time. In 1889, Congress divided the Dakota Territory in half, and North Dakota became the 39th state of the Union in November of that year. Following statehood, the population increased quickly, and by 1910 it had reached almost 600,000.

The Great Depression of the 1930s hit North Dakota especially hard, since the state also suffered a devastating drought. During World War II, the economy recovered, as farmers provided much food for the U. S. troops. The discovery of oil near Tioga in 1951 and the construction of Garrison Dam near Riverdale between 1946 and 1960 gave an additional boost to the economy.

Today, agriculture continues to be important, as North Dakota strives to encourage industrial growth within its borders.

Sports

Many sporting events on the collegiate and secondary school levels are played throughout the state. In hockey, the University of North Dakota won the NCAA championship in 1959, 1963, 1980, 1982, and 1987.

Major Cities

Bismarck (population 44,485). Settled in 1873, the town was named in honor of Germany's chancellor in an effort to attract German investors for the railroad. The capital city of North Dakota, which lies on the east bank of the Missouri River, developed into an important riverboat port and railway

The spirit of the West is alive at Frontier Village in Jamestown, where visitors can see a collection of 19th-century buildings.

terminal. Since the first oil well opened in 1951, Bismarck has become a center for this growing industry.

Things to see in Bismarck: State Capitol, North Dakota Heritage Center, State Historical Museum, Statue of Sakakawea, Camp Hancock State Historic Site, Riverside-Sertoma Park, Dakota Zoo, Double Ditch Indian Village, and E'lan Art Gallery.

Fargo (population 61,383). Founded in 1872, North Dakota's largest city is located in the fertile Red River Valley. It is a leading commercial center of the Northwest. The city, named for William G. Fargo of the Wells Fargo Express Company, became important as a supply point for settlers headed west. Many of Fargo's hotels feature casinos run by charities and nonprofit organizations.

Things to see in Fargo: Roger Maris Baseball Museum, and Bonanzaville, USA.

Places to Visit

The National Park Service maintains three areas in the state of North Dakota: Theodore Roosevelt National Park, Knife River Indian Villages National Historic Site, and part of Fort Union Trading Post National Historic Site. In addition, there are 12 state recreation areas.

Bottineau: International Peace Garden. Located in the Turtle Mountains on both sides of the United States-Canadian border, this complex is a tribute to the friendship of the two nations.

Devils Lake: Fort Totten State Historic Site. The 1867 fort, built to protect settlers headed for Montana, contains many of the original buildings.

Grand Forks: Myra Museum and Campbell House. The museum, featuring artifacts from the late-19th century, shares the grounds with the 1879 log cabin home of agricultural innovator Tom Campbell.

Jamestown: Frontier Village. The "World's Largest Buffalo," a three-story statue of an American bison, is the main feature of this complex, which also contains many restored buildings.

Mandan: Fort Abraham Lincoln State Park. The reconstructed

North Dakota

Commanding Officer's Quarters, the home of General George A. Custer from 1873-76, is located on the park grounds.

Minot: Roosevelt Park and Zoo. The 28-acre zoo is situated in a park featuring gardens, a swimming pool, and the "Magic City Express," a replica of a Great Northern steam locomotive.

Rugby: Geographical Center Pioneer Village and Museum. The village, which features 27 restored buildings, stands at the geographical center of the North American continent.

Events

There are many events and organizations that schedule activities of various kinds in the state of North Dakota. Here are some of them.

The United Tribes Pow-Wow celebrates North Dakota's Native American heritage.

Sports: Badlands Circuit Finals Rodeo (Bismarck), McQuades Softball Tournament (Bismarck), Sports Camp (Bottineau), Roger Maris Celebrity Golf Tournament (Fargo), Governor's Walleye Cup Derby (Garrison), State Hockey Tournament (Grand Forks), Potato Bowl (Grand Forks), Fort Abraham Lincoln Great American Horse Race (Mandan), Rodeo Days (Mandan), Champions Ride Rodeo (Sentinel Butte), Winter Carnival (Williston).

Arts and Crafts: Summerthing (Grand Forks), Spring Craft Show (Jamestown), Art in the Park (Mandan), Country Fair (Rugby).

Music: Summer Pops Series (Bismarck), International Music Camp (Bottineau), Phil Patterson Bandshell Concerts (Dickinson), International Old Time Fiddlers' Contest (Dunseith), Medora Musical (Medora), Frost Fire Musical (Walhalla), Band Day (Williston).

Entertainment: Missouri River Expo (Bismarck), Missouri Valley Fair (Bismarck), United Tribes Pow-Wow (Bismarck), Folkfest (Bismarck), Waterski Carnival (Bottineau), Steam Thresher Show (Carrington), Carrington Folkfest (Carrington), Fort Totten Days (Devils Lake), Roughrider Days Celebration (Dickinson), Pioneer Days (Dickinson), Northern Plains Ethnic Festival (Dickinson), Heritage Hjemkomst Festival (Fargo), Merry Prairie Christmas (Fargo), Sodbuster Days (Fort Ransom), Native American Annual Time Out and Wacipi (Grand Forks),

Potato Bowl Week (Grand Forks), Stutsman County Fair (Jamestown), Buffalo Days (Jamestown), Frontier Army Days (Mandan), Winter Daze (Mandan), North Dakota State Fair (Minot), Norsk Hostfest (Minot), Little Shell Powwow (New Town), Turtle Mountain Pow-Wow Celebration (Rolla), State Championship Horse Show (Rugby), North Dakota Winter Show (Valley City), Community Days (Valley City), Fort Buford 6th Infantry State Historical Encampment (Williston), Fort Union Trading Post Rendezvous (Williston), Buffalo Trails Day (Williston), Samlingfest (Williston).

Tours: Lewis and Clark Riverboat (Bismarck), Dakota Queen Riverboat (Grand Forks), Yard and Garden Tour (Hatton), Fort Seward Wagon Train (Jamestown).

Theater: Fort Totten Little Theatre (Devils Lake), LaMoure Summer Theatre (Grand Rapids).

Famous People

Many famous people were born in the state of North Dakota. Here are a few:

Fred G. Aandahl 1897-1966, Litchville. U.S. government official

Lynn Anderson b. 1947, Grand Forks. Country and pop singer

Angie Dickinson b. 1931, Kulm. Television and film actress: *Police Woman, Dressed to Kill*

Roy Sarles Durstine 1886-1962, Jamestown. Advertising executive

Carl Ben Eielson 1897-1929, Hatton. Bush pilot

John B. Flannagan 1895-1942, Fargo. Sculptor

Croil Hunter 1893-1970, Fargo. Airline executive

Louis L'Amour 1908-88, Jamestown. Novelist

William Langer 1886-1959, near Everest. Senate leader

Peggy Lee b. 1920, Jamestown. Pop singer

Pete Retzlaff b. 1931, Ellendale. Football player

Eric Sevareid b. 1912, Velva. Newscaster

Ann Sothern b. 1909, Valley City. Television and film actress: *The Ann Sothern Show, The Whales of August*

Lawrence Welk b. 1903, near Strasburg. Bandleader

Colleges and Universities

There are many colleges and universities in North Dakota. Here are the more prominent, with their locations, dates of founding, and enrollments.

Dickinson State College, Dickinson, 1918, 1,402

Jamestown College, Jamestown, 1884, 841

Mary College, Bismarck, 1959, 1,431

Mayville State College, Mayville, 1889, 764

Minot State College, Minot, 1913, 3,304

North Dakota State University, Fargo, 1890, 9,432

University of North Dakota, Grand Forks, 1883, 12,210

Valley City State College, Valley City, 1889, 1,140

Where To Get More Information

Tourism Promotion Division
Economic Development Commission
Liberty Memorial building
600 E. Boulevard Avenue
Bismarck, ND 58505
1-800-437-2077

South Dakota

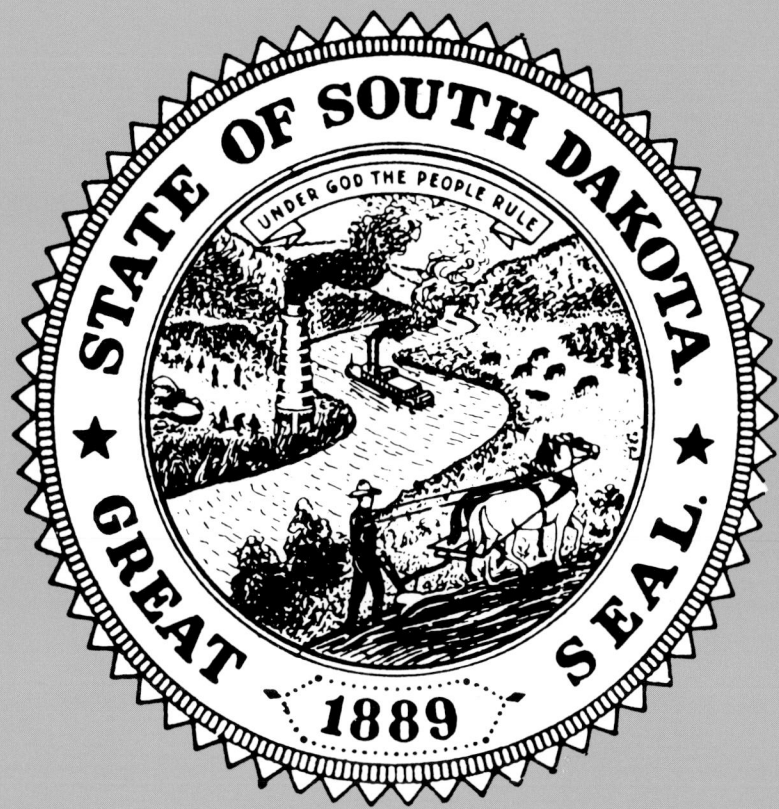

The state seal of South Dakota, adopted in 1889, depicts a landscape with a farmer plowing, a steamboat on the river, a smelter furnace, and cattle grazing in a field of corn. Hills can be seen in the distance, and the state motto appears on a scroll at the top. The border inscription reads "State of South Dakota, Great Seal" and "1889," the year the state joined the Union.

State Flag

South Dakota has two official state flags. The first, adopted in 1909, contains the state seal on one side and the sun on the other. Because of the expense involved in manufacturing a two-sided flag, a second was adopted in 1963. It consists of the state seal surrounded by a yellow sunburst and the words "South Dakota—The Sunshine State," centered on a sky blue field.

State Motto

Under God the People Rule
This motto, originally adopted in 1885, was suggested by Dr. Joseph Ward, founder of Yankton College.

The 60-foot-high faces of Mount Rushmore grace the majestic Black Hills.

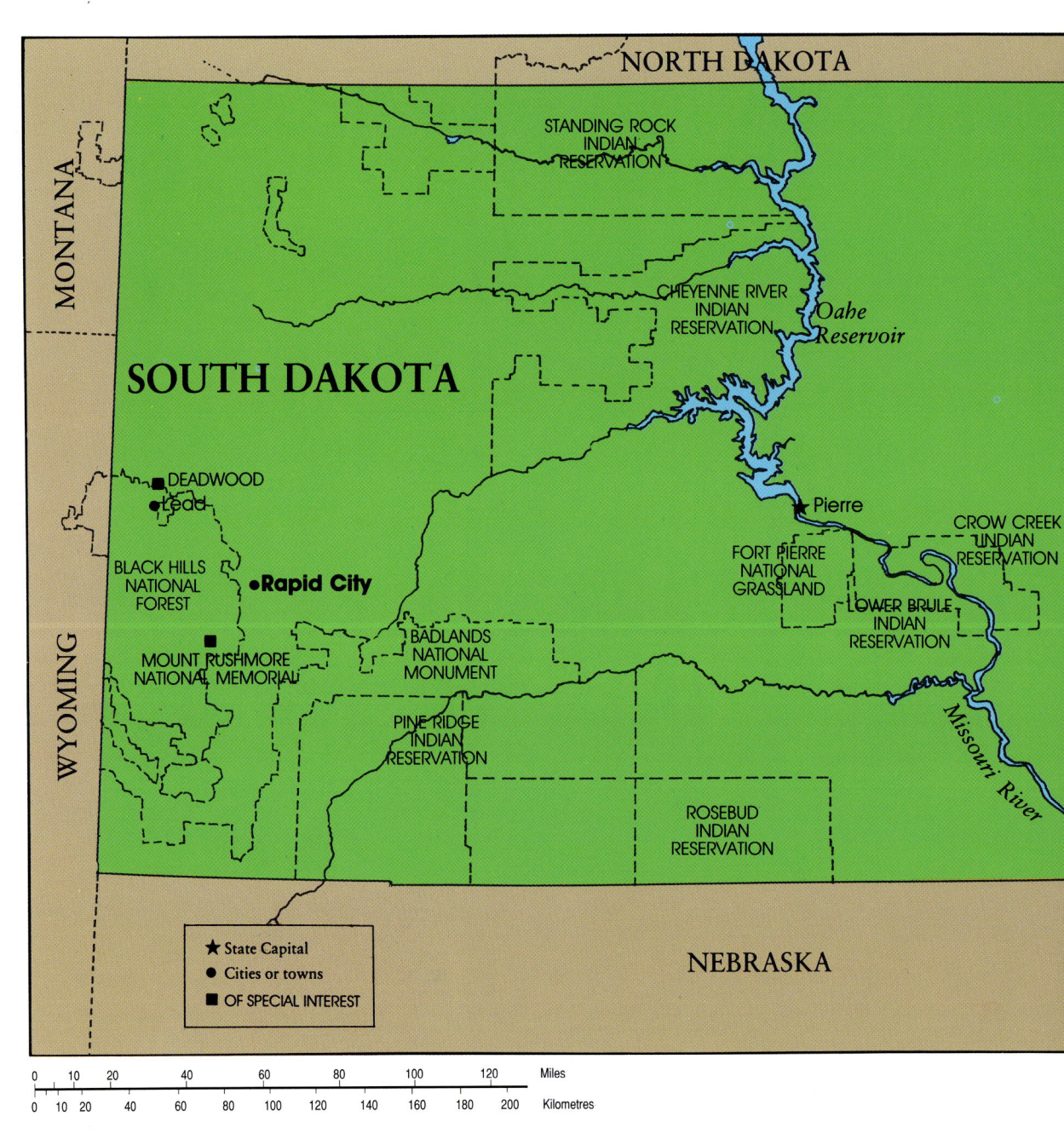

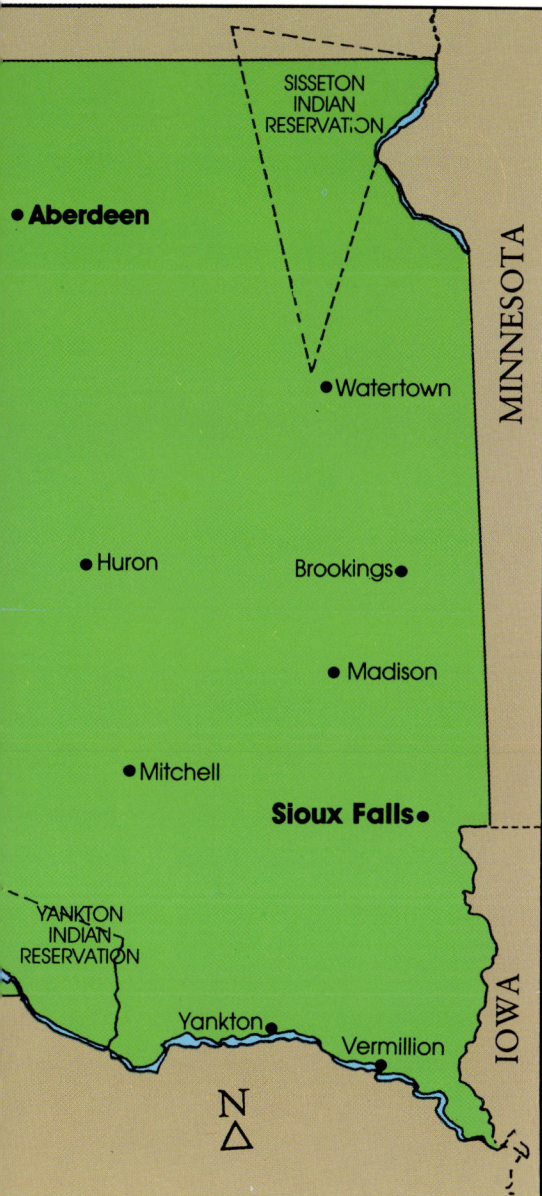

The capitol in Pierre was built in 1910 and restored in 1989.

State Capital

Pierre was selected as the temporary capital when South Dakota became a state in 1889. It was named the permanent capital in 1904. Construction on the capitol building was begun in 1907 and completed in 1910, at a cost of $1 million. Built of limestone and white marble, the structure is topped by a dome reaching a height of 156 feet and covered with 40,000 pounds of copper. The pillars around the rotunda are made of scagliola, an imitation marble composed of glue, gypsum, and dye. An inner dome of leaded stained glass rises 96 feet above the mosaic floor.

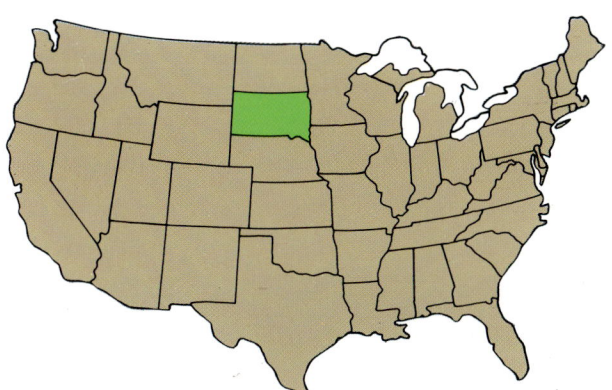

South Dakota

State Name and Nicknames

The name South Dakota came from the Sioux Indians of the region, who called themselves *Dakota* or *Lakota*, meaning "allies" or "friends."

South Dakota is nicknamed the *Sunshine State* because of its sunny climate. It has also been called the *Coyote State* for its many coyotes. Other nicknames include the *Blizzard State* because of its harsh winters and the *Artesian State* for its many artesian wells.

State Flower

The American pasque

The state flower is the American pasque.

The ring-necked pheasant is the state bird.

flower, *Pulsatilla hirsutissima*, was chosen state flower in 1903.

State Tree

The Black Hills spruce, *Picea glauca densata*, was adopted as state tree in 1947.

State Bird

In 1943, the ring-necked pheasant, *Phasianus colchicus*, was named state bird by the legislature.

State Animal

The coyote was designated state animal in 1949.

State Fish

The walleye, *Stizostedion vitreum*, was selected state fish in 1982.

State Gem

In 1966, fairburn agate was chosen state gem.

State Grass

Western wheat grass, *Agropyron smithii*, was adopted state grass in 1970.

State Insect

The honeybee, *apis mellifera*, was named state insect in 1978.

State Mineral

Rose quartz was selected state mineral in 1966.

State Song

"Hail, South Dakota," words and music by Deecort Hammitt, was adopted state song in 1943.

Population

The population of South Dakota in 1990 was 699,999, making it the 45th most

South Dakota

populous state. There are 9.1 people per square mile—46.4 percent of the population live in towns and cities.

Geography and Climate
Bounded on the north by North Dakota, on the east by Minnesota and Iowa, on the south by Nebraska, and on the west by Wyoming and Montana, South Dakota has an area of 77,116 square miles, making it the 16th largest state. The climate features extreme temperatures, persistent winds, and low precipitation and humidity. The major land areas include the Prairie Plains in the east, the Great Plains in the west, and the Black Hills in the west-central part of the state. The highest point, at 7,242 feet, is Harney Peak in Pennington County, and the lowest point, at 966 feet, is along Big Stone Lake in Roberts County. The major waterways are the Cheyenne, Grand, Big Sioux, James, Missouri, Moreau, Vermillion, Bad, and

Needles Highway was built to showcase the striking rock formations of the Black Hills.

White rivers. Lake Oahe, which was formed by the Oahe Dam, is the largest lake in South Dakota.

Industries
The principal industries of the state are agriculture, manufacturing, and services. The chief manufactured products are food and food products, machinery, and electric and electronic equipment.

Agriculture
The chief crops of the state are corn, oats, wheat, sunflowers, soybeans, and sorghum. South Dakota is also a livestock state; there are estimated to be 3.4 million cattle, 1.7 million hogs and pigs, and 590,000 sheep on its farms. Ponderosa pine is harvested. Gold and Portland cement are important mineral resources.

Government
The governor is elected to a four-year term, as are the lieutenant governor, secretary of state, attorney general, commissioner of school and public lands, treasurer, and auditor. The state legislature, which meets annually, consists of a 35-member senate and a 70-member house of representatives. Voters in each of the 35 legislative districts elect one senator and two representatives for two-year terms.

The most recent state constitution was adopted in 1889. In addition to its two United States senators, South Dakota has one representative in the U.S. House of Representatives. The state has three votes in the electoral college.

History

Three major Indian tribes inhabited present-day South Dakota before the Europeans arrived. The Arikara lived near the mouth of the Cheyenne River and along the Missouri River. The Cheyenne occupied the land near the western part of the Cheyenne River, along the White River and in the Black Hills. The Sioux, also called the Dakota, followed the buffalo herds across the region.

In 1743, Canadian explorers François and Louis-Joseph La Vérendrye became the first white men to visit the South Dakota area. The region was included in the Louisiana Purchase of 1803, when France sold the Louisiana Territory to the United States. The following year, Meriwether Lewis and William Clark explored the area on their way to the Pacific Ocean. The first permanent settlement in the region was a fur-trading post built by Joseph La Framboise in 1817 at present-day Fort Pierre. The fur trade, aided by steamboat travel on the Missouri River, flourished until 1850, when the number of fur-bearing animals decreased and the demand for fur diminished.

In 1861, Congress established the Dakota Territory, comprised of North and South Dakota and part of Montana and Wyoming. Several Indian wars occurred during South Dakota's territorial years. The Red Cloud War, the most important of these, ended with the signing of the Laramie Treaty in 1868. In 1874, the federal government sent General George A. Custer to investigate reports of gold in the Black Hills,

Soldiers line up at Fort Sisseton, where frontier military history is brought to life during a festival each June.

South Dakota

thus violating the treaty. The soldiers confirmed the reports, and many prospectors rushed to the area. Richer deposits discovered in 1876 near present-day Lead and Deadwood brought another flood of gold seekers. Indian uprisings resulted, but in a new treaty later that year the Indians gave up their claims to the Black Hills. The last fighting in South Dakota took place at Wounded Knee Creek in 1890, during which 200 Indian men, women, and children were killed.

After 1870, the population increased, numbering 348,600 by 1890. Urged by citizens of the territory, Congress set the boundary between North and South Dakota in 1889. Later that year, South Dakota was admitted to the Union as the 40th state.

World War I brought prosperity to the state. Prices of farm products increased and farmland doubled in value. In 1930, South Dakota was hit by a severe drought and a grasshopper plague that, together with the Great Depression, caused a decrease in population. To help provide jobs for farmers, the federal government established the Civilian Conservation Corps and the Works Progress Administration.

During World War II, South Dakota farmers used machinery to help boost their food production, resulting in unemployment for many farmworkers. In 1944, Congress approved the Pick-Sloan Missouri Basin Program, which provided for the construction of four hydroelectric dams on the Missouri River. The lakes created by the dams, known as the "Great Lakes of South Dakota," attracted tourists, giving rise to the state's second largest industry.

Today, South Dakota is trying to decrease its dependence on agriculture by attracting industry with its liberal tax laws, clean air, and low-cost electric power.

Sports

Many sporting events on the collegiate and secondary school levels are played throughout the state. In addition, hiking, fishing, and water sports are also popular.

Although the state does not have any professional teams in the major sports leagues, the Rapid City Thrillers and the Sioux Falls Skyforce are members of the Continental Basketball Association, the

One of the best trout streams in the Black Hills rolls through Spearfish Canyon.

official developmental league of the National Basketball Association.

Major Cities

Rapid City (population 46,492). Founded in 1876, two years after the discovery of gold in the Black Hills, Rapid City is the second largest city in the state. Tourism, mining, lumbering, and agriculture support the local economy.

Things to see in Rapid City: Sioux Indian Museum and Crafts Center, Minnilusa Pioneer Museum, Dahl Fine Arts Center, Dinosaur Park, South Dakota School of Mines and Technology, Museum of Geology, Stage Barn Crystal Cave, Black Hills Petrified Forest, Crystal Cave Park, Sitting Bull Crystal Cave, Black Hills Caverns, Marine Life Aquarium, Story Book Island, Black Hills Reptile Gardens, Thunderhead Underground Falls, Chapel in the Hills, Ellsworth Air Force Base, and Bear Country, USA

Sioux Falls (population 81,492). Originally founded in 1856, the town was abandoned six years later because of the threat of Indian attacks. It was reestablished in 1865 and prospered, especially after the arrival of the railroad in the late 1800s. Today, it is a center for banking, meat packing, medical care, and agriculture.

Things to see in Sioux Falls: Pettigrew Home and Museum, Old Courthouse Museum, E.R.O.S. Data Center, Sherman Park, Great Plains Zoo, Delbridge Museum of Natural History, Indian Mounds, USS *South Dakota* Battleship Memorial, Civic Fine Arts Center/Museum, and the Center for Western Studies.

Places to Visit

The National Park Service maintains four areas in the state of South Dakota: Mount Rushmore National Memorial, Jewel Cave National Monument, Wind Cave National Park, and Badlands National Park. In addition, there are 29 state recreation areas.

Custer: National Museum of Woodcarving. The museum

Mammoth Site in Hot Springs holds one of the largest collections of prehistoric elephant fossils in the Western Hemisphere.

features life-size animated figures by Dr. Niblack, one of the original animators of Disneyland.

Deadwood: Ghosts of Deadwood Gulch Wax Museum. More than 70 wax figures portray historic scenes in the settlement of South Dakota.

De Smet: Laura Ingalls Wilder Memorial. Guided tours of this area include the author's childhood home and many

South Dakota

other buildings referred to in her books.

Hot Springs: Mammoth Site. This excavation site contains the largest known concentration of mammoth bones in the Western Hemisphere.

Huron: Gladys Pyle Historic Home. This Queen Anne style house, built around 1894, was the home of the first woman elected to the U.S. Senate.

Keystone: Rushmore-Borglum Story and Gallery. Exhibits include original models and tools used by Gutzon Borglum in sculpting Mount Rushmore.

Lead: The Homestake Gold Mine. Visitors may tour the surface workings of one of the largest operating gold mines in the Western Hemisphere.

Mitchell: Enchanted World Doll Museum. This museum—a castle with a drawbridge, moat, and stained-glass windows—houses more than 4,000 dolls arranged in scenes from fairy tales and story books.

Pierre: South Dakota Discovery Center and Aquarium. Hands-on exhibits in many areas allow visitors to discover and experiment with science.

Spearfish: Classic Auto Museum. Exhibits include more than 100 antique and classic cars dating from 1908 to the 1960s.

Events

There are many events and organizations that schedule activities of various kinds in the state of South Dakota. Here are some of them.

Sports: Black Hills Roundup (Belle Fourche), State Fair Speedway (Huron), Corn Palace Stampede Rodeo (Mitchell), Greyhound Racing at Black Hills Greyhound Track (Rapid City), Black Hills Motorcycle Classic (Sturgis), Pro-Bowl Rodeo (Watertown), Elks Rodeo (Winner).

Arts and Crafts: Summer Festival (Brookings), Meadowood Arts Fair (Huron), Black Hills Gold (Rapid City), Sioux Pottery and Crafts (Rapid City), Black Hills Pow Wow and Arts Expo (Rapid City), Northern Plains Tribal Arts (Sioux Falls).

Music: Mountain Music Show (Custer), Fife and Drum Corp Concerts (Hill City), South Dakota and Open Fiddling Contest (Yankton).

Entertainment: Snow Queen Festival (Aberdeen), Little International (Brookings), Gold Discovery Days (Custer), Fall Festival (Custer), Days of '76 (Deadwood), Heart of the Hills Celebration (Hill City), Huron Air Show (Huron), South Dakota State Fair (Huron), Steam Threshing Jamboree (Madison), Corn Palace Festival (Mitchell), Corn Palace Polka Festival (Mitchell), Oglala Nation Fair and Rodeo (Pine Ridge), Black Hills Heritage Festival (Rapid City), Central States Fair (Rapid City), Rosebud Sioux Tribal Affairs and Powwow (Rosebud), Sioux Empire Fair (Sioux Falls), Fort Sisseton Historical Festival (Sisseton), Antique Auto Festival (Sisseton), Black Hills Sawdust Day (Spearfish), Spring Festival (Sturgis), Steam and Gas Threshing Bee (Sturgis), Kampeska Days (Watertown), Wildlife Festival (Watertown), Day County Fair (Webster), Heritage Days (Yankton), Riverboat Days (Yankton).

Tours: Native American Loop (Chamberlain), Jeep Ride to Buffalo (Custer), Pickler Mansion (Faulkton), 1880 Train (Hill City), Homestake Gold Mine Surface Tours (Lead).

Theater: Trial of Jack McCall for the Murder of Wild Bill Hickok (Deadwood), Laura Ingalls Wilder Pageant (Huron), Black Hills Passion Play (Spearfish), Lewis and Clark Playhouse (Yankton).

Famous People

Many famous people were born in the state of South Dakota. Here are a few:

Sparky Anderson b. 1934, Bridgewater. Baseball manager

Floyd Bannister b. 1955, Pierre. Baseball pitcher

Tom Brokaw b. 1940, Webster. Television journalist

Dave Collins b. 1952, Rapid City. Baseball player

Hallie Flanagan 1890-1969, Redfield. Playwright

Joe Foss b. 1915, near Sioux Falls. Governor, military hero, and American Football League president

Gall 1840-94, on Moreau River. Indian leader

Philip L. Graham 1915-63, Terry. Journalist and publisher

John Grass 1837-1918, near Grand River. Indian leader

Edith Green 1910-87, Trent. Congresswoman

Alvin Hansen 1887-1975, Viborg. Economist

Mary Hart b. 1951, Sioux Falls. Television host: *Entertainment Tonight*

Hubert Humphrey 1911-78, Wallace. Vice-President and Senate leader

Cheryl Ladd b. 1951, Huron. Television and film actress: *Charlie's Angels*

Ernest O. Lawrence 1901-58, Canton. Nobel Prize-winning physicist

George McGovern b. 1922, Avon. Senate leader and presidential candidate

Earl Sande 1898-1968, Groton. Jockey

Carl L. Schmidt 1885-1946, Brown County. Biochemist

Sitting Bull 1834-90, on Grand River. Indian leader

Norm Van Brocklin 1926-83, Eagle Butte. Hall of Fame football quarterback

Colleges and Universities

There are many colleges and universities in South Dakota. Here are the more prominent, with their locations, dates of founding, and enrollments.

Augustana College, Sioux Falls, 1860, 2,004

Black Hills State College, Spearfish, 1883, 2,412

Dakota State College, Madison, 1881, 1,224

Mount Marty College, Yankton, 1922, 917

Northern State College, Aberdeen, 1901, 3,100

Oglala Lakota College, Kyle, 1970, 890

Sioux Falls College, Sioux Falls, 1883, 962

South Dakota School of Mines and Technology, Rapid City, 1885, 2,156

South Dakota State University, Brookings, 1881, 7,080

University of South Dakota, Vermillion, 1862, 6,397

Where To Get More Information

Department of Tourism
Capitol Lake Plaza
Pierre, SD 57501
1-800-843-1930

Wyoming

The seal of the state of Wyoming, adopted in 1893, shows a woman standing on a pedestal holding a banner containing the state motto. Male figures on each side of the pedestal represent the mining and livestock industries. The dates 1869 and 1890, which appear below the pedestal, are the years that Wyoming became a territory and a state. "Great Seal of the State of Wyoming" is printed in the border.

State Flag
The state flag of Wyoming, adopted in 1917, contains the state seal in the center of the white silhouette of a buffalo on a blue field. The flag is enclosed by a white inner border, which stands for purity, and a red outer border, which represents the blood of the pioneers and the Indians.

State Motto
Equal Rights
The state motto, officially adopted in 1955, refers to the fact that in 1869, Wyoming became the first state to give women the right to vote.

Winter lays claim to Yellowstone Park.

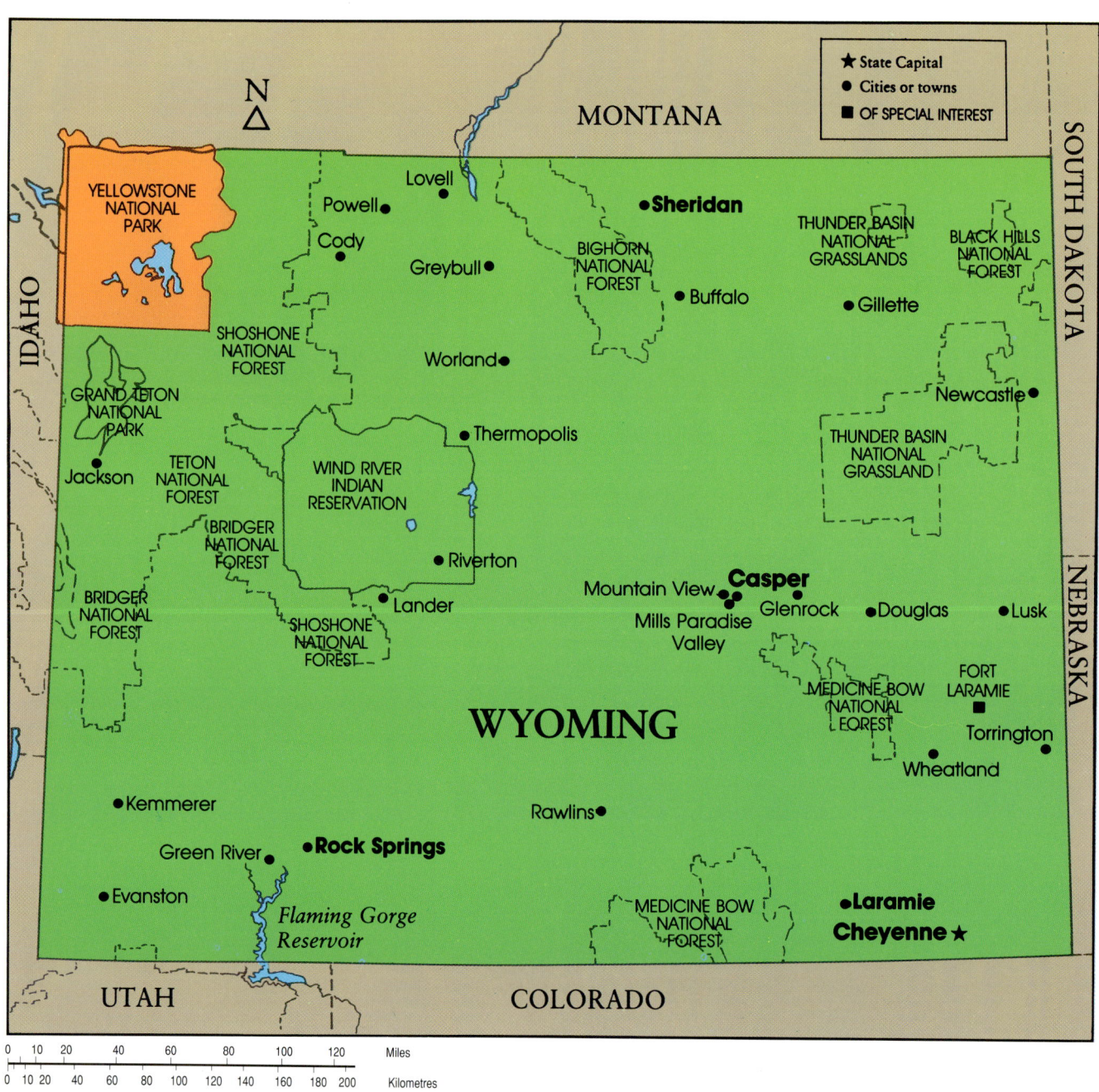

Wyoming

The state capitol in Cheyenne was designed by D. W. Gibbs in 1887, three years before Wyoming became a state.

State Capital

Cheyenne became the territorial capital of Wyoming in 1869 and continued as state capital after Wyoming was admitted to the Union in 1890. The Corinthian-style, sandstone building, which serves as the statehouse, resembles the United States Capitol. Completed in 1890, the structure has a gold-leafed dome that reaches a height of 145 feet. New east and west wings were added to the building between 1915 and 1917. The total cost of the capitol, including its additions, was $389,569.

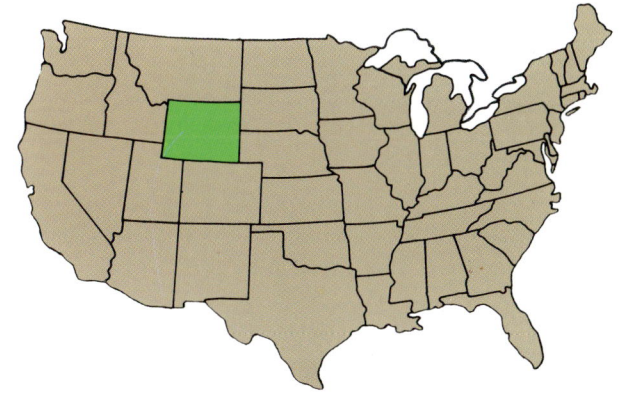

The meadowlark is the state bird.

State Name and Nicknames
The name Wyoming comes from the Delaware Indian word *mecheweamiing*, which means "upon the great plain."

Wyoming is often called the *Equality State* because it was the first state to give women the right to vote. Other nicknames include the *Cowboy State* and *Big Wyoming*.

State Flower
Indian paintbrush, *Castilleja linariaefolia*, was chosen state flower in 1917.

State Tree
The plains cottonwood, *Populus sargentii*, was named state tree in 1947 and again in 1961.

State Bird
In 1927, the meadowlark, *Sturnella neglecta*, was selected state bird.

State Gemstone
Jade was designated state gemstone in 1967.

State Mammal
The American bison, *Bison americanus*, was adopted state mammal in 1985.

State Song
"Wyoming," with words by Charles E. Winter and music in two versions, one by George E. Knapp, and one by Earle R. Clemens, was named state song in 1955.

Population
The population of Wyoming in 1990 was 455,975, making it the 50th most populous state. There are 4.7 people per square mile—62.7 percent of the population live in towns and cities.

Geography and Climate
Bounded on the north by Montana, on the east by South Dakota and Nebraska, on the south by Colorado and Utah, and on the west by Utah, Montana and Idaho, Wyoming has an area of 97,809 square miles, making it the ninth largest state. The climate is cool and dry, with wide-ranging daily temperatures and little rainfall. The Great Plains meet the Rocky Mountains in Wyoming, and the Continental Divide cuts diagonally across the state. The highest point, at 13,804 feet, is Gannett Peak in Fremont County, and the lowest, at 3,099 feet, is along the Belle Fourche River in Crook County. The major waterways are the Yellowstone, Bighorn, Tongue, Belle Fourche, Laramie, Powder, Cheyenne, Niobrara, North Platte, Green, Snake, Bear, Wind, and Shoshone rivers. The

Wyoming

state's largest natural lake is Yellowstone Lake.

Industries

The principal industries of the state are mineral extraction, tourism and recreation, and agriculture. The chief manufactured goods are refined petroleum products, foods, wood products, stone, clay, and glass products.

Agriculture

The chief crops of the state are wheat, beans, barley, oats, sugar beets, and hay. Wyoming is also a livestock state; there are estimated to be 1.38 million cattle, 16,000 hogs and pigs, and 837,000 sheep on its farms. Aspen and yellow pine are harvested. Portland cement and crushed stone are important mineral resources.

Government

The governor is elected to a four-year term, as are the secretary of state, auditor, treasurer, and superintendent of public instruction. The state legislature, which meets annually, consists of a 30-member senate and a 64-member house of representatives. Senators serve four-year terms, and representatives serve two-year terms. The most recent state constitution was adopted in 1889, and has been amended over 50 times. In addition to its two United States senators, Wyoming has one representative in the U. S. House of Representatives. The state has three votes in the electoral college.

History

Indians hunted in the Wyoming area at least 11,000 years ago. When the Europeans arrived, the Arapaho, Bannock, Blackfeet, Cheyenne, Crow, Flathead, Nez Percé, Shoshone, Sioux, and Ute tribes inhabited the region.

Exploration of present-day Wyoming did not begin until after the Louisiana Purchase of 1803, in which the United States bought most of the area from France. In 1807, John Colter, a fur trapper, explored the Yellowstone area, discovering its geysers and hot springs. A group of fur traders led by Robert Stuart discovered South Pass—a route across the Rocky Mountains—in 1812, making westward travel easier. Another group led by Captain L. E. de Bonneville discovered oil in the Wind River Basin in 1833. A year later, the first permanent trading post, Fort William, was established by William Sublette and Robert Campbell. Wyoming belonged to the territories of Louisiana, Missouri, Nebraska, Oregon, Washington, Idaho, Utah, and Dakota at various times in its history. Spain owned part of southern Wyoming until the 1800s. It became part of the United States when Texas joined the Union in 1845.

Many settlers passed through Wyoming on their

way west. Upset by their arrival, the Plains Indians raided the wagon trains. The attacks lessened after Indian leaders signed a peace treaty with the U. S. Army in 1868. That same year, Congress established the Territory of Wyoming. A year later, the territorial legislature gave women the right to vote and hold public office, becoming the first in the nation to do so. During the territorial years, cattle ranching and gold mining increased in importance. The first oil well was drilled in the Dallas Field, and tourism got its start when Yellowstone became the first national park. Wyoming entered the Union as the 44th state in 1890.

Disputes over cattle rustling escalated into the Johnson City War in 1892. Federal troops had to be called in to put an end to the turmoil.

After 1900, the population grew rapidly as a result of the Homestead acts of 1909, 1912, and 1916, which provided

Built in 1834, Fort Laramie was the earliest permanent white settlement in Wyoming.

free land for settlers. The Great Depression of the 1930s did not affect Wyoming as badly as other states. Increased oil production and government construction projects, including the Alcova and Seminoe dams, helped the state's economy. Demands for coal, lumber, meat, and oil during World War II also contributed to the state's economic health. In 1951, large uranium deposits were discovered near the Powder River. The United States government opened its first long-range missile base near Cheyenne in 1960.

Today, the state is trying to attract new industries while maintaining its place as a leading producer of coal and petroleum.

Sports

Many sporting events on the collegiate and secondary school levels are played throughout the state. In football, the University of Wyoming won the Gator Bowl in 1951, and the Sun Bowl in 1956, 1958, and 1966.

Wyoming

The school also won the NCAA basketball championship in 1943.

Major Cities

Casper (population 49,600). Founded in 1888, Casper became an oil town when the first well was drilled in 1889. The demand for oil during World War I brought prosperity to the town. Today, tourism, agriculture, and mining have joined oil as the city's major industries.

Things to see in Casper:
Fort Casper Museum, Natrona County Pioneer Museum, Nicolaysen Art Museum and Discovery Center, Werner Wildlife Museum, Edness K. Wilkins State Park, Casper Mountain and Beartrap Meadow Parks, Lee McCune Braille Trail, Alcova Lake Park, and Dan Speas Fish Hatchery.

Cheyenne (population 50,900). Founded in 1867, Wyoming's largest city is also the state's capital. It quickly developed a reputation as Hell on Wheels because of the gunmen, gamblers, and confidence men who operated there. It is the retail and banking center of the region. Cattle and sheep ranching, coal, oil, and timber are important industries.

Things to see in Cheyenne:
State Capitol, Historic Governors' Mansion State Historic Site, State Museum and Art Gallery, Warren Air Force Base, National First Day Cover Museum, Cheyenne Frontier Days Old West Museum, Holiday Park, Wildlife Visitor Center, and Curt Gowdy State Park.

Places to Visit

The National Park Service maintains eight areas in the state of Wyoming: Yellowstone National Park, Grand Teton National Park, Devils Tower National Monument, Fossil Butte National Monument, Fort Laramie National Historic Site, Bighorn Canyon Recreation Area, Flaming Gorge Recreation Area, and Thunder Basin National Grassland. In addition, there are ten state recreation areas.

Alcova: Independence Rock State Historic Site. The names of more than 5,000 pioneers are carved into this 193-foot-high granite boulder.

Buffalo: Johnson County-Jim Gatchell Memorial Museum. Dioramas in this museum depict events in local history, including the Johnson County Cattle War.

Cody: Buffalo Bill Historical Center. The four museums that comprise the center detail the art, crafts, culture, and history of the American West.

Douglas: Wyoming Pioneer Memorial Museum. The museum features a large collection of pioneer and Indian artifacts from the 1800s.

Jackson: Aerial Tramway. The two-and-a-half-mile ride carries visitors to the top of Rendezvous Mountain, 10,450 feet above sea level.

Laramie: Laramie Plains Museum. Housed in a restored Victorian mansion, the museum features period furnishings.

Medicine Bow: Como Bluff Fossil Cabin. The cabin, constructed entirely of dinosaur bones, features a museum containing rocks and artifacts of the area.

Newcastle: Anna Miller Museum. The museum displays antique firefighting equipment and pioneer memorabilia.

Riverton: Riverton Museum. This museum features Shoshone and Arapaho costumes, and demonstrations of pioneer skills, such as silversmithing and quilting.

Sheridan: Bradford Brinton Memorial-Museum and Historic Ranch. The 20-room main house contains works of art by American artists Charles M. Russell and Frederic Remington, among others.

Events

There are many events and organizations that schedule activities of various kinds in the state of Wyoming. Here are some of them.

Sports: Polo matches (Big Horn), Central Wyoming Fair Race Meet (Casper), Casper Classic Bicycle Races (Casper), Cody Stampede (Cody), Cody Nite Rodeo (Cody), Cowboy Days (Evanston), Para Ski Championships (Jackson), Jackson Hole Rodeo (Jackson), Old-Timer's Rodeo (Lander), One Shot Antelope Hunt (Lander), Pack Horse Race (Pinedale), Pen-to-Pen Run (Rawlins), Rocky Mountain All-Girl Rodeo (Rock Springs), Flaming Gorge Fishing Tournament (Rock Springs), Red Desert Round-up (Rock Springs), Saratoga Ice Fishing Derby (Saratoga), Sheridan-Wyo PRCA Rodeo (Sheridan), Silver Bullet Bike Race (Worland).

Arts and Crafts: Jackson Hole Fall Arts Festival (Jackson), Mountain Artist's Fest Rendezvous (Jackson), Saratoga Craft Fair (Saratoga).

Music: Grand Teton Music Festival (Jackson), Grand Targhee Music Festival (Jackson), State Championship Old-time Fiddle Contest (Riverton), Cowboy Music and Poetry Festival (Riverton).

Entertainment: Lincoln County Fair (Afton), Bozeman Trail Days (Buffalo), Buffalo Merchants Crazy Days (Buffalo), Christmas Parade (Buffalo), Central Wyoming Fair and Rodeo (Casper), Cottonwoods Festival (Casper), Cheyenne Frontier Days (Cheyenne), Western Plains Fair (Cheyenne), Buffalo Bill Birthday Celebration (Cody), Frontier Festival (Cody), Main Street Festival (Cody), Plains Indians Powwow (Cody), Jackalope Days (Douglas),

The rodeo brings the Wild West to Wyoming every year in towns like Jackson Hole and Cody.

Wyoming

Wyoming State Fair (Douglas), Winter Carnival (Dubois), Buffalo Barbeque (Dubois), Wind River Rendezvous (Dubois), Chili Cook-off (Evanston), Uinta County Fair (Evanston), Mountain Man Rendezvous (Evanston), Bridger Valley Pioneer Days (Fort Bridger), Fort Bridger Rendezvous (Fort Bridger), Flaming Gorge Days (Green River), Days of '49 Celebration (Greybull), Covered Wagon Cookout and Wild West Show (Jackson), Wyoming Winter Fair (Lander), Pioneer Days (Lander), Jubilee Days (Laramie), Elizabethan Fair (Laramie), Laramie River Rendezvous (Laramie), Mustang Days (Lovell), Medicine Bow Days (Medicine Bow), Whoop 'n Holler Days (Newcastle), Winter Carnival (Pinedale), Wyoming Wheels Weekend (Pinedale), Indian Powwows (Riverton), Sweetwater County Fair (Rock Springs), Sierra Madre Winter Carnival (Saratoga), Goshen County Fair (Torrington), Dad Worland Days (Worland), Washakie County Fair (Worland).

Tours: Wyoming River Trips (Cody), Wild West Jeep Tours (Jackson), Wagon Treks (Jackson), Fort Jackson Float Trips (Jackson).

Theater: Gertrude Krampert Summer Theatre (Casper), Atlas Theater (Cheyenne), Jackson Hole Playhouse (Jackson), Pink Garter Theater (Jackson), Dirty Jack's Wild West Theater and Opera House (Jackson), Green River Rendezvous (Pinedale), Legend of Rawhide Pageant (Lusk), Variety Theatre (South Pass City), Gift of the Waters Pageant (Thermopolis),

Famous People

Many famous people were born in the state of Wyoming. Here are a few:

Thurman W. Arnold 1891-1969, Laramie. U.S. assistant attorney general

Tom Browning b. 1960, Casper. Baseball pitcher

Don Cockroft b. 1945, Cheyenne. Football player

Mike Devereaux b. 1963, Casper. Baseball player

Boyd Dowler b. 1937, Rock Springs. Football player

June Etta Downey 1884-1932, Laramie. Psychologist and author

Dick Ellsworth b. 1940, Lusk. Baseball pitcher

Curt Gowdy b. 1919, Green River. Broadcaster

Jerry Hill b. 1939, Torrington. Football player

Jackson Pollock 1912-56, Cody. Artist

Alan K. Simpson b. 1931, Cody. Senate leader

Howard M. Snyder 1881-1970, Cheyenne. U.S. Army officer and physician

Spotted Tail 1833-81, near Fort Laramie. Indian leader

James Watt b. 1938, Lusk. U.S. Secretary of the Interior

Colleges and Universities

There are several colleges and universities in Wyoming. Here is the most prominent, with its location, date of founding, and enrollment. *University of Wyoming*, Laramie, 1886, 10,994

Where To Get More Information

Wyoming Division of Tourism
I-25 at College Drive
Cheyenne, WY 82002
1-800-225-5996

Bibliography

General

Aylesworth, Thomas G. and Virginia L. *Let's Discover the States: The Great Plains*. New York: Chelsea House, 1988.

Montana

Carpenter, Allan. *Montana*, rev. ed. Chicago: Childrens Press, 1979.

Fradin, Dennis B. *Montana in Words and Pictures*. Chicago: Childrens Press, 1981.

Lang, William L. and Myers, R. C. *Montana: Our Land and People*. Boulder, CO: Pruett, 1979.

Malone, Michael P. and Roeder, R. B. *Montana: A History of Two Centuries*. Seattle: University of Washington Press, 1976.

Nebraska

Carpenter, Allan. *Nebraska*, rev. ed. Chicago: Childrens Press, 1979.

Creigh, Dorothy Weyer. *Nebraska: A Bicentennial History*. New York: Norton, 1977.

Fradin, Dennis B. *Nebraska in Words and Pictures*. Chicago: Childrens Press, 1980.

Nebraska: A Guide to the Cornhusker State. Lincoln, NE: University of Nebraska Press, 1979.

North Dakota

Carpenter, Allan. *North Dakota*, rev. ed. Chicago: Childrens Press, 1979.

Fradin, Dennis B. *North Dakota in Words and Pictures*. Chicago: Childrens Press, 1981.

Tweton, D. Jerome and Jelliff, Theodore. *North Dakota: The Heritage of a People*. Fargo, ND: North Dakota Institute for Regional Studies, North Dakota State University, 1976.

Wilkins, Robert P. and Huchette, Wynona. *North Dakota: A Bicentennial History*. New York: Norton, 1977.

South Dakota

Carpenter, Allan. *South Dakota*, rev. ed. Chicago: Childrens Press, 1978.

Fradin, Dennis B. *South Dakota in Words and Pictures*. Chicago: Childrens Press, 1981.

Milton, John R. *South Dakota: A Bicentennial History*. New York: Norton, 1977.

Schell, Herbert S. *History of South Dakota*, 3rd ed. Lincoln, NE: University of Nebraska Press, 1975.

Wyoming

Bailey, Bernadine. *Picture Book of Wyoming*, rev. ed. Whitman, 1972.

Bragg, William F. *Wyoming: Rugged But Right*. Boulder, CO: Pruett, 1980.

Carpenter, Allan. *Wyoming*, rev. ed. Chicago: Childrens Press, 1979.

Fradin, Dennis B. *Wyoming in Words and Pictures*. Chicago: Childrens Press, 1980.

Lamb, Russell. *Wyoming*. Portland: Graphic Arts Center, 1978.

Larson, Taft A. *Wyoming: A Bicentennial History*. New York: Norton, 1977.

Index

A
American Fur Company, 11
Arapaho Indians, 11, 21, 57
Arikara Indians, 34, 46
Assiniboin Indians, 11, 34
Atsina Indians, 11

B
Bad River, 45
Badlands, *33*
Bannock Indians, 11, 57
Bear River, 56
Belle Fourche River, 56
Big Blue River, 21
Big Sioux River, 45
Big Stone Lake, 45
Bighorn River, 56
Billings (MT), 13
Bismarck (ND), 31, *31*, 35
Bitterroot River, 11
Black Hills, *41*, 45, *45*, 46, 47, *47*
Blackfeet Indians, 11, 57
Bonneville, Captain L. E. de, 57

C
Campbell, Robert, 57
Cannonball River, 33
Casper (WY), 59
Cavelier, Robert, 22, 34
Cheyenne (WY), 55, *55*, 58, 59
Cheyenne Indians, 11, 12, *12*, 21, 34, 57
Cheyenne River, 45, 46, 56
Chippewa Indians, 34
Clark River, 11
Clark, William, 11, 22, 35, 46
Clemens, Earle R., 56
Cody (WY), 59, *60*
Cohen, Charles, C., 10
Colleges and Universities (MT), 14; (NE), 26; (ND), 38; (SD), 50; (WY), 61
Colter, John, 57
Comanche Indians, 21
Coronado, Francisco Vásquez de, 22
Crow Indians, 11, 57
Custer, George A., 12, *12*, 46

D
Dakota Indians, 46
Devils Lake, 33, *34*
Drift Prairie, 33

E
Elkhorn River, 21

F
Famous People (MT), 14; (NE), 25-26; (ND), 38; (SD), 50; (WY), 61
Fargo (ND), 36
Flathead Indians, 57
Flathead Lake, 11
Flathead River, 11
Foley, James W., 32
Ford River, 11
Fort Atkinson, 22
Fort Benton, 11
Fort Laramie, *58*
Fort Pierre, 46
Fort Sisseton, *46*
Fort Totten, *34*
Fort William, 57
Fox Indians, 22
Fras, Jim, 20
Frontier Village, *36*

G
Gannett Peak, 56
Garrison Dam, 35
Gibbs, D. W., *55*
Glacier National Park, *7*, 12
Goose River, 33
Grand River, 45
Granite Peak, 11
Grasshopper Creek, 12
Great Britain, 12
Great Depression, 12, 22, 35, 47, 58
Great Plains, 11, 21, 33, 45, 56
Green River, 56

H
Harney Peak, 45
Hammitt, Deecort, 44
Heart River, 33
Helena (MT), 9, *9*, 13
Hidatsa Indians, 34
Homestead Act, 22
Hot Springs, *48*, 49
Howard, Joseph, E., 10

I
Iowa Indians, 22

J
Jackson Hole (WY), *60*
James River, 33, 45
Jamestown (ND), *36*
Johnson City War, 58

K
Kalispel Indians, 11
Knapp, George E., 56
Knife River, 33
Kootenai River, 11
Kutenai Indians, 11

L
La Framboise, Joseph, 46
La Vérendrye, François, 46
La Vérendrye, Louis-Joseph, 46
Lake McConaughty, 21
Lake Oahe, 45
Lake Sakakawea, *29*
Laramie River, 56
Laramie Treaty, 46
Lewis, Meriwether, 11, 22, 35, 46
Lincoln (NE), 18, *18*, 23, *23*, *25*
Little Bighorn River, 12
Little Blue River, 21
Little Missouri River, 33
Louisiana Purchase, 12, 46
Loup River, 21

M
Mammoth Site, *48*
Mandan Indians, 11, 34, 35
Marias River, 11
Milk River, 11
Miller, Guy G., 20
Missouri Indians, 21
Missouri River, 5, 11, 21, 33, 45, 46, 47
Moreau River, 45
Mount Rushmore, *41*
Musselshell River, 11

N
National Czech Festival, *25*
Needles Highway, *45*
Nez Percé, 11, 57
Niobrara River, 21, 56
North Platte River, 21, 56
Northern Pacific Railway, 13

O
Oahe Dam, 45
Omaha (NE), 24
Omaha Racers, 23
Omaha Indians, 21
Oregon Trail, 22, *22*
Oto Indians, 21

P
Pacific Ocean, 35, 46

Index

Park County, 11
Park River, 33
Pawnee Indians, 21
Pembina River, 33
Pierre (SD), 43, *43*
Pike, Zebulon M., 22
Plains Indians, 58
Platte River, 20, 21, 22, *23*
Ployhar, James D., 32
Ponca Indians, 21
Powder River, 11, 56, 58
Putnam, C. S., 32

R
Rapid City (SD), 48
Rapid City Thrillers, 47
Red Cloud War, 46
Red River Valley, 33
Red River, 33
Republican River, 21
Rocky Mountains, 11, 15, 56, 57

S
Salish Indians, 11
Santee Sioux Indians, 22
Sauk Indians, 22
Sheyenne River, 33
Shoshone Indians, 11, 57
Shoshone River, 56
Sioux Falls (SD), 48
Sioux Falls Skyforce, 47
Sioux Indians, 11, 12, *12*, 21, 32, 34, 46, 57
Snake River, 56
Souris River, 33
South Platte, 21
Spearfish Canyon, 47

State animal (MT), 10; (NE), 20; (SD), 44; (WY), 56
State art gallery (ND), 32
State beverage (ND), 32
State bird (MT), 10, *10*; (NE), 20; (ND), 32, *32*; (SD), 44, *44*; (WY), 56, *56*
State capital (MT), 9, *9*; (NE), 18, *18*; (ND), 31, *31*; (SD), 43, *43*; (WY), 55, *55*
State day (NE), 20
State fish (MT), 10; (SD), 44
State flag (MT), 7, *7*; (NE), 17, *17*; (ND), 29, *29*; (SD), 41, *41*; (WY), 53, *53*
State flower (MT), 10; (NE), 20, *20*; (ND), 32, *32*; (SD), 44, *44*; (WY), 56
State fossil (NE), 20; (ND), 32
State gems (MT), 10; (NE), 20; (SD), 44; (WY), 56
State grass (MT), 10; (NE), 20; (ND), 32; (SD), 44
State insect (NE), 20; (SD), 44
State march (ND), 32
State mineral (SD), 44
State motto (MT), 7; (NE), 17; (ND), 29; (SD), 41; (WY), 53
State name and nicknames (MT), 10; (NE), 20; (ND), 32; (SD), 44; (WY), 56
State rock (NE), 20
State seal (MT), 5, *5*; (NE), 15, *15*; (ND), 27, *27*; (SD), 39, *39*; (WY), 51, *51*
State slogan (MT), 10; (NE), 20
State soil (NE), 20
State songs (MT), 10; (NE), 20; (ND), 32; (SD), 44; (WY), 56
State tree (MT), 10; (NE), 20; (ND), 32; (SD), 44; (WY), 56
Stuart, Robert, 22, 57

Sublette, William, 57
Sun River, 11

T
Tongue River, 56

U
United Tribes Pow-Wow, 37
University of Nebraska, 23, 26
University of North Dakota, 35, 38
University of Wyoming, 58, 61
Ute Indians, 57

V
Varennes, Pierre Gaultier de, 35
Vermillion River, 45

W
Ward, Joseph, 41
White Butte, 33
White River, 45, 46
Williston Basin, 12
Wind River Basin, 57
Wind River, 56
Winnebago Indians, 22
Winter, Charles E., 56
World War I, 47
World War II, 12, 23, 35, 47, 58
Wounded Knee Creek, 47

Y
Yankton College, 41
Yellowstone Lake, 57
Yellowstone Park, *53*, 59
Yellowstone River, 11, 56, 57, 58

Photo Credits/Acknowledgments

Photos on pages 6-7 (Steve Bly), 9, 10, 12, courtesy of Travel Montana Department of Commerce; pages 16-17, 20, 22, 23, 25, courtesy of Nebraska Department of Economic Development; pages 28-29, 31, 32, 33, 34, 36, 37, courtesy of North Dakota Tourism Promotion Division; pages 40-41, 43, 44, 45, 46, 47, 48, courtesy of South Dakota Office of Tourism; pages 52-53, 55-56, 58, 60, courtesy of Wyoming Division of Tourism; pages 3 (top), 5, courtesy of Montana Secretary of State; pages 3 (middle), 15, courtesy of Nebraska Secretary of State; pages 3 (bottom), 27, courtesy of North Dakota Secretary of State; pages 4 (top), 39, courtesy of South Dakota Secretary of State; pages 4 (bottom), 51, courtesy of Wyoming Secretary of State.

Cover photograph courtesy of North Dakota Tourism Promotion Division (Ken Jorgensen)

BROADVIEW PUBLIC LIBRARY DISTRICT
2226 SOUTH 16TH AVENUE
BROADVIEW, ILLINOIS 60153
(708) 345-1325